IT'S A DOABLE DEAL!

A "Knights" battle with Cancer

Rachel Susan Knight

All rights reserved. No part of this book is to be reproduced without the written consent of the author and publisher, except by a reviewer who may quote brief passages in review. The author guarantees all contents are original and do not infringe upon the legal rights of any other person or work.

The views expressed in this book do not necessarily represent those of M. Publications or any affiliates. The author and publisher disclaim any responsibility for any liability, loss, and or risk, personal or otherwise, which may be incurred as consequences directly or indirectly related to the contents of this book.

Copyright © 2011- 978-0-9829326-5-0

Published by M. Publications LLC
P.O Box 327
Roanoke, TX 76262

Cover Design By: Fletcher Graphics LLC.

Dedication

This book is dedicated to Alexis Leeann.
You'll always be your Mommy's little princess.

Follow me as I blog my way through my third bout with Cancer before age 25. I am just your average wife and mother - except that I have no hair, spend way more time throwing up than I should, and these days I fight Cancer in my free time. (It isn't the most pleasant hobby, but it makes for good reading!)

Sunday, July 11, 2010

What is this all about?

I guess to start off we will get into the basics of who I am and what this blog is all about. My name is Rachel Knight. I am a 23 year-old wife and mother to one little five year old. Another part of who I am is a Cancer patient. I was diagnosed with Acute Lymphoblastic Leukemia on July 31st, 2001, when I was fourteen years old. After my initial treatment I was in clinical remission up until I relapsed in March 2008.

Approximately two weeks ago, I finished up all of the treatment scheduled on my relapse protocol. At the end of treatment, I had scans and a biopsy of my bone marrow to ensure that there were no traces of leukemia blast cells present in my system so we could officially declare that I was again in remission. Unfortunately, the bone marrow biopsy revealed my worst fear, that my leukemia was not gone. It appears as though my leukemia became resistant to the chemotherapy I was taking, and now our only option for treatment is a bone marrow transplant.

A bone marrow transplant is a very scary thing, and something I am not very familiar with. What I do know is that it will require many weeks in the hospital, multiple doses of very intense chemotherapy, and time away from my job, family, friends, and simply my life as I know it; it will change drastically for quite some time.

I intend to use this blog to update all of my friends and family on what I am doing throughout the course of treatment. This will be my own outlet for feelings and different things I want to share with all of you while I am away.

Posted by Rachel at 9:52 AM

10

Monday, July 12, 2010

Ready or not, here it comes.

We just got home from our meeting with the doctor this whole thing is rather overwhelming to say the least. It looks like it all begins tomorrow and there is no turning back. I will go in tomorrow and start a five-week regimen of chemotherapy. This is a stronger dose of chemo than I've ever had and it's designed to completely destroy all of the cells in my bone marrow, both cancerous and healthy. The plan will hopefully go like this: I will be in the hospital for about five days getting chemo, then I will come home and wait for my counts to recover. This should take anywhere from 2-4 weeks. Once my blood counts recover I will have another bone marrow biopsy. If the amount of cancer cells in my bone marrow is less than 0.1% at that time, we will proceed with transplant; that is if I have a bone marrow donor by then. We are thinking sometime in early August. As far as the actual details of the transplant, I guess that will come tomorrow when I meet with the transplant coordinator. They will also begin work on finding a donor match, which includes my sister being tested and adding me to the National Bone Marrow Registry.

From what I can gather, I will be sicker than I can imagine. There are a lot of moving parts to make sure this thing works like it needs to. I have faith that this will all work out. I know that I will suffer a lot in all of this, but that at the end of the day I will be a happy healthy person again soon.

I will try to update again tomorrow after I meet with the transplant coordinator and get settled into the hospital. I am sure I will be bombarded with loads of information in the next few days, and I will make sure to pass it along.

Posted by Rachel at 4:41 PM

Wednesday, July 14, 2010

Not much to say, but better than saying nothing.

I guess nothing too exciting has been going on around here, but I figure I better not go without updating when I can so that you all don't worry about me. My mom and I have been going over different ideas for fundraisers and such. Whatever we do, hopefully that will be one less thing to worry about. I'm amazed at all the different ideas that people have and who is willing to help. We are truly blessed. My sister got tested to see if she would be my marrow donor today, and we should know the results by next week.

So far the chemotherapy they are giving me is making me very exhausted and not really able to eat. I had about two sips of chicken noodle soup since breakfast yesterday and that was about all I could take without getting sick.

I got a lot of books and information about transplants from the transplant coordinator yesterday, and I haven't read any of it. I guess there will be plenty of time for that later.

I am sorry this post is all over the place, but like I said before – I am kind of out of it this morning.

Posted by Rachel at 2:17 PM

Thursday, July 15, 2010

Day 3 of 5

Well, today is chemo day three. In a couple of hours I will receive another round of chemo and then sleep until tomorrow. That seems to be the pattern I am following, at least I ate a little bit of dinner last night, but that's all since I've been here, really. Luckily all of the sleeping is keeping my mind off of the fact that this place sucks and it smells terrible. I wish I could wash my sheets at least twice a day; they start to smell like latex rather quickly.

My aunt's wedding is in a few days and I am really starting to get bummed out that I can't be there. I was supposed to be in the wedding, and now even if I am feeling up to it, there are no guarantees I'll be out of the hospital in time to even see it. I am just trying to remind myself, as I will have to a lot in the coming year, that once this is all over with I can leave this Cancer thing behind me once and for all. This is my cure, my future, my hope.

Lexi is still having a good time with Grandma and Papa, so that makes me feel better too. She is my heart, and when she is happy, I am happy.

I wish I had more to update but unfortunately that's all that is going on right now. We are patiently waiting over the next few days to see if my sister will be my donor, and once we get the results from that we will know what is next: either a worldwide marrow search or a meeting to decide how soon I can get into transplant.

I met my social worker today. She seemed very nice and hopefully helpful. She is going to look into a few possible options for me to get grants or things to help with the bills since I will be out of work longer than my disability will cover. That would be nice, not to mention my husband can take time off to be with me up to twelve weeks, but not paid. It would be rough not having him by my side throughout the transplant. However, it would be even rougher if we didn't have a home to come back to either. I am not too worried about it though because I know it will all work out. I can just feel it. Stressing about it won't do any good either.

Posted by Rachel at 12:06 PM

Friday, July 16, 2010

Is it okay?

Is it okay that I don't like today?
That I wish I were home, curled up in my bed on this certainly miserable day?

Is it okay that I am not strong today?
That I am trying to hold back tears in every way?

Is it okay that I wish tomorrow was today?
That on this day, I don't want to come out and play?

Is it okay that I'm tired today?
That I'm not a fighter, but only a survivor on this certainly miserable day?

Posted by Rachel at 7:38 AM

2 for 1

Well, I guess today can be a 2 for 1 day; two posts in one day. It's been a pretty blah day. My stomach has been upset and I am having a hard time sleeping because of it, which makes me cranky. My husband has been busy getting our house ready for me to come home this weekend but that means he is gone from me for several hours at a time, which makes me cranky as well. I did take a short nap after he left and before my dad got here (for the shift change), and woke up to a sweet card from Ryan and April.

Ryan is my husband's cousin and April is a very good friend of his. Both are very sweet people and it really brightened my day to have the card lying on my bed after my nap. Then after my dad got here, one of the new oncologist's came in to talk to me. She was really nice and asked me a lot of questions about what kinds of things they could get for me to do while I am here that would peak my interest. I really hope that turns into something. It would be nice to have more to do than read Blue's Clues books and watch PG movies while I am in here for a transplant. I guess we shall see.

Right now I am just taking it one step at a time and I'm ready to get this week over with. I am praying that this goes as planned and I will be home on Sunday in my comfy bed with my fluffy puppy, my husband, and my little girl. I know I have a LONG road ahead of me, but one day at a time and through the sheer grace of GOD we will get through it. I have no doubt.

Hope everyone has a good Friday night!)

Posted by Rachel at 6:26 PM

Saturday, July 17, 2010

No sleeping in today.

It's 6:06 am on a Saturday morning and I am wide awake! Is it because I have to work in a few hours? Nope. Is it because I have a newborn baby to get up with? Nope. Oh yeah, it's because I am stuck in the hospital with a terrible stomachache and I wish I was just about anywhere else but here. Never fear though, my nurse just brought me a delicious fruit punch Gatorade/MiraLax mixture. For those of you who don't know MiraLax is to help you poop. Hey, chemo doesn't equal glamorous, sorry. If all goes as planned I should get to go home sometime tomorrow, that would be nice. I need to pet my puppy.

I'm sure that today will be a lot like yesterday except I think my husband will be able to stay all day with me, which is good. I don't do well without him, but he knows that. After I type this I will probably "nap" for a few more hours, wake up and call my mom. She will come see me, brief me on my crazy family's activities over the last 24 hours and then march out of here with purpose. (She always has a purpose, what can I say.) Dad will come see me this afternoon, which is always nice. Dad doesn't bother me, ever. He lets me stare at the ceiling for five hours and not say a word if I want, but he will talk to me until I fall asleep if that's what I want. Dads, or at least my dad, are amazing.

Maybe I will eat twice today, that is my goal. Everyone has goals right?

Well, it's super early so you may hear from me again later today, if I can think of something witty to write.

Posted by Rachel at 6:06 AM

Incredible who?

I think at first glance, it's easy to say in order to beat Cancer you need to be strong, very strong. Some of the strongest people I know are Cancer survivors and that is wonderful. What I have learned in the past couple of days about strength and fighting Cancer is that you can in fact be too strong. In a normal circumstance "too strong" doesn't really exist, but here I promise it does. It wasn't until I was getting comments, e-mails, and phone calls from everyone that heard about my relapse telling me how strong I was. However, it was my husband who took me in his arms and told me exactly what everyone wasn't telling me. He told me I didn't have to be strong and that this could kick my ass in every way; that I could be as weak as I wanted to be and that was just fine. He said I could be strong only if I felt like it, but if I couldn't be strong, then he would be strong for me.

It took a few days for that to set in because at first it sounds kinda' silly. What do you mean if I want to be strong? I HAVE to be strong or this thing wins, right? Wrong. You see, for the past nine years (yeah, its been that long) I have made the mistake of trying to be too strong. Sometimes when you have a weak day, you tend to feel like you've failed. When you're getting chemo you get weak and there is nothing you can do about it. Your body will start to shut down, and you WILL weaken. It usually takes a few months for it to bother me, but that weakness is where my defeat starts. Normally, it would be my will and desire to be strong and to show everyone that I've got this. This time, I know better. I DON'T have this, but that's okay with me. Will I beat this? Of course. I'll go nine more years if I have to, but I AM weaker than this medicine and I WILL crumble. I'll crumble right into the arms of my husband. When I am weak, he will be my strength. I have unfortunately made the mistake of being too strong for my own good sometimes, but not this time.

Thank you baby for showing me that this is not a war I am fighting alone, and that being weak and falling apart is all part of putting myself back together.

Posted by Rachel at 10:44 PM

Sunday, July 18, 2010

Not so fast.

I almost let today get away without an update. I was sitting here thinking about how all of you are at home waiting patiently for my update - with nothing else to do with your time, so I owed it to you. Oh wait, I am the one stuck at home with nothing to do but update all of you. I got it backward...Ha-ha!

Today has been a strange day I guess you can say. First and foremost, I am home from the hospital (Hallelujah, let the Angel's sing!). I started my day off by waking up REALLY early in order to have a lengthy discussion with my nurse about my "laxative" options and oh, getting my blood drawn. (Even a slight headache when you're on a lot of chemotherapy sends the entire staff into an uproar and they feel the need to do nine thousand tests.) Blood counts were fine and my headache was more than likely due to the fact that I had a loud beeping machine hooked up to me while I tried to sleep for the past five days, or at least that is my best guess. ANYWAY, I then wasted the next eight hours doing random things around the hospital room until it was time to go. Jason Witten, a Dallas Cowboy, was at the hospital before I left so that was cool. I actually had my Cowboys hat with me so I got it signed and took a picture with him. They said they would e-mail it to me...we will see.

Great news! I finally get to go home and I couldn't be happier. When I arrived I noticed that my house was spotless, my fridge was packed, and my Nana was here. Well today is my aunt's wedding and I am bridesmaid...well, supposed to be. I must admit I was pretty bummed out though when everyone had to pack up and leave for the wedding. Unfortunately, my pretty dress is still in the closet wrapped up. My shoes, well David's Bridal will be calling me soon to come and get them I assume. Claire, you will just have to take me out dancing in my dress as soon as I am better.

My baby girl is here and I missed her badly. She didn't quite miss me yet though, she was still trying to find a way to go to Grandma and Papa's tonight. Oh well, at least I know she loves them and will have no problem on her extended stay with them.

I ate a ton today, which is always good. I think my husband is proud of me for that. I never know when or what I can eat from day to day, so in the words of the King of Pop - "Don't stop 'till you get enough!"

All right, all right - enough of my pointless banter for one night. Thanks for reading my little blog. Goodnight!

Posted by Rachel at 10:41 PM

Monday, July 19, 2010

You win!

Orange Juice: 1, My Esophagus: 0

Ugh...

Posted by Rachel at 3:22 AM

Just another day.

Today has been for the most part, uneventful. Of course when fighting Cancer, that's a good thing. I haven't had a great day, but I've been worse. I have pretty much been in bed or lying around. I just can't seem to nail down any one thing I need to do. My mind is starting to have trouble focusing on even the simplest tasks. I went through this last time, so it is to be expected. I just feel a little helpless. Thankfully my husband knows this though and he lets me tinker around the kitchen and walk back to the living room as many times as I want until I get over tired, then he just sends me up to my bed. My mom and Nana were here this morning and they've had Lexi all day. I am glad they took her to do something because I have had a miserable headache all day while my husband installed Corbin's new doggie door.

I was able to take a bath in my own bathtub with no tubes today. I got the water too hot and had to recover from that for a while, but it was still worth it. Hopefully my night will consist of dinner and a lot of sleep. I am exhausted!

Here's to another boring day tomorrow, maybe without the headache!

Posted by Rachel at 6:48 PM

Wednesday, July 21, 2010

Business as usual...sorta.

Lexi came home a little while ago. My husband is working on filling holes in the back yard and I am lying in bed using my laptop. I love days like today. Days like today remind me why I wake up every day to fight this all over again. It's because I have an amazing husband who loves Lexi and I more than I could ever know someone could. It's because I have a precious little girl with the most beautiful curls anyone has ever seen. It's because my puppy, who looks more like a rat after an unfortunate grooming visit, gets so happy to see me every time we let him out of the kennel in the morning, just because.

I have been having trouble catching my breath for the past couple of days, and after a bunch of tests and a breakdown in the doctor's office today, we think it's anxiety related. Which is good, I think. Anxiety is manageable.

Physically I'm a mess. I have no white blood count, which means I am stuck at home in strict isolation. Thank you Dr. Shawn for those orders. I can't really get out of bed to do anything without getting dizzy. I've had a terrible headache for three days, which is probably from my spinal tap, and my stomach is quite certainly in no less than 713 knots, BUT - I am here.

Oh, and I just ate a hot dog from Celio's!)

Posted by Rachel at 1:04 PM

To Lexi,

I found this letter today while I was cleaning out some old e-mails. It's a letter I wrote to my daughter in '07. She was 2 years old then.

One day when you are all grown up and you are a mom of your own, this may make more sense to you. I wish I could find words to tell you how much you mean to me. I never knew until I held you for the first time what true love was. You are the reason why I breathe every day. I could not imagine my life without you in it. You give everything I do for the rest of my life purpose. I know that God created me to be your mother. That is my whole reason for existence, and there is nothing in the world that can compare to you. You fill my heart with more joy than I ever knew the world had to offer. You are my baby girl and my precious gift from God. I will spend my every waking moment trying to protect you from harm. I know there will come times when I make you mad, or I might not make the best decisions, but I will ALWAYS love you with everything I have to offer. You are a part of me; you are my blood, sweat and tears. There is nothing I wouldn't do for you, and no matter what happens in this life, know that NOBODY will ever come first in my life over you. Alexis LeeAnn, I love you with all of me; mind, body and soul!

Posted by Rachel at 1:34 PM

Friday, July 23, 2010

A few pics I love, and an update.

My daughter Lexi, and my husband Shawn had a date night. They went to the Cheesecake Factory and saw a movie. I gave her some money and my husband said she paid for everything and even pulled the seat down for him at the movie theater. I love those two so much!

We got the results back from my sister's bone marrow typing test today. It looks like she is not a match. They will now be doing a worldwide search of the Bone Marrow Registry in order to find the best match available. By mid next week we should know the results.

I am kind of bummed about it, but I know that in the end it will all work out, one way or another. I have been doing a lot of research and talking to many different transplant survivors over the Internet, and more often than not they have matched unrelated donors. The way I look at it is like this; sure, ideally my sister would be my perfect 10/10 match, but in an ideal world I would never have had Cancer to begin with. So we deal with it, fix only what we can, and move on.

In other news, nothing exciting is going on and that is great. Excitement usually involves going to the hospital. I am starting to develop some mouth sores, so I have to be careful of what I eat; nothing abrasive like chips or cereal for a few days. I got my Magic Mouthwash from the doctor so that helps. (Yes, it is actually called "Magic Mouthwash," says it right on the prescription bottle.)

I hope everyone has a happy weekend. I hear that actually means something out in the real world. For me, the weekend means that the clinic is closed and if I get sick I have to go to the E.R. Ick!

Posted by Rachel at 2:42 PM

Marrow Matters

I have had a lot of people ask me how they can be tested to see if they are a match to be my bone marrow donor. I appreciate every offer, but it is unfortunately much more complicated than that. First of all, the hospital will only test my full blood siblings. That's why my sister was tested. Even my parents are at best a 50% match, which isn't enough for transplant unless it is the only possible option. The only other way to be considered is through the National Marrow Donor Program. If you go today and get tested, you will be an active part of the registry in about six weeks. The search for my marrow match has already started and we should have the results in a few days. Since they are hoping to have me in transplant by early August, any new donors would take too long to be processed. Luckily, because I am a small size they also have told me that they can look to the cord blood registry as well; which is even more promising.

Just for a side note, the traits that they look for in a bone marrow match are actually 10 different proteins and there is about a 1 in 20,000 chance that a particular person is a 10/10 match. I've been told blood type has nothing to do with this, and even gender doesn't matter. So, besides the time restriction, the odds of finding someone who I know that also happens to be a close enough match for transplant is slim to none.

I DO encourage everyone to consider joining the registry though. Not for me, but for anyone around the world that might need it. Bone marrow is something that you grow back in a couple weeks and finding a good match is so important to a successful transplant that you could really save a life. You can visit National Marrow Donor Program - Be The Match Marrow Registry to find out more.

Lastly, on very, very rare occasion, I have heard of patients who were unable to find suitable matches through the registry doing a personal marrow drive. This would be a last resort for me, and a decision made by my oncologist. If it did come down to that, trust me, you'll know.

Thank you everyone for the support. It means so much to me!

Posted by Rachel at 11:21 PM

Sunday, July 25, 2010

Thought I forgot about you, huh?

Since I am getting close to missing two days in a row, I figured I better buckle down and put in an update. I have just been so busy the past few days it's been hard to find the time. Okay, who am I kidding; I have really done nothing but watch TV and play on the internet. I just didn't have anything to say.

As far as how I am doing physically, I have surprised even myself with how well I'm doing. I do have to take it easy because each day I get a little more light-headed when I walk around, due to the fact that my blood counts are decreasing. Also, last night and today I have started having some deep bone pain. This is most likely a side effect from the injection I got last Sunday to help boost my white blood cells when they start to grow back. I like to think of it as "cell fertilizer!" In case you're looking this stuff up, it's called Neulasta.

I have a doctor's appointment in the morning for blood work, and will possibly get a blood transfusion. If I do end up needing a transfusion (which they seem pretty sure I will), I will be there all day and most of the day Tuesday. Oh, Joy!

I am extremely pleased with the fact that I am still home. They used the phrase "If you're not in the hospital by then" several times last week when referring to scheduling my appointment for tomorrow, so the doctors fully expected I would spike a fever sometime over the past four days, and I haven't! (Knock on wood)
I don't know what I am expecting to find out tomorrow at the clinic, but here's to good news!

Goodnight!

Posted by Rachel at 9:48 PM

Monday, July 26, 2010

Nice!

I had my doctor's appointment this morning at 9am. First off, I got there and realized that my appointment was actually at 8am, so I was an hour late. Whoops! They still saw me right away though, which was nice.

They did blood work and had me wait on the results to see if we needed to come back this afternoon. Turns out my counts were great and I don't have to get blood! I am still on the low side with everything and have to be careful, but not so low that I need a transfusion. So, they assumed I would be in the hospital; I'm sitting at home on the couch. They assumed I would need a few transfusions; I haven't needed one. They assumed it would take a few weeks for my counts to start recovering; it's been eight days. Am I good or what?)

Now, I have a follow up on Thursday and I will have another bone marrow biopsy sometime in the next week to see if the leukemia cells responded to my treatment, or if we face another round of chemotherapy before we are ready to do transplant.

Posted by Rachel at 1:19 PM

34

Tuesday, July 27, 2010

Is counting sheep a hobby?

I am so excited. I got to spend the morning with my niece, Sophia. I absolutely love her and was happy to see her. I think tomorrow we trade and her twin brother, my nephew Carson, comes to visit.

My husband is back at work today so my mom is now on duty. She brought me breakfast, made a deposit in the bank for me, and entertained Lexi so I didn't lose my mind. That pretty much covers what is involved in taking care of me right now. I have a giant (ok, it's tiny but it hurts like its giant) sore on the side of my tongue so I have to be careful what I eat. I ate some acidic fruit last night and it irritated my mouth some. I am trying to force myself to stay in bed today so that I will nap. Now that I know my body is working so hard to boost my blood counts, I want to rest and do whatever I can to help.

I think the extreme boredom is setting in today. I can only check my e-mail and play Bejeweled for so long. Nothing comes on TV during the day that I am into except The Food Network, and I just get mad because I can't cook right now. I started rifling through Amazon.com and wrote down a few books I would like to read, and I think my mom is going to check out Hobby Lobby for a few crafts. Oh well, as long as I am bored in my own bed and not in the hospital. This situation could always be a lot worse!

Posted by Rachel at 3:06 PM

Wednesday, July 28, 2010

Wow!

Wow. I really, really don't even know how to begin my post today, but we'll give it a whirl. I am realizing a lot of people are reading my blog so I need to watch my spelling and punctuation, or, I could just blame it on "Chemo-brain" and move on. I got some Tetris to play.

Today has been filled with very little boredom. My nephew Carson came over for a few hours and I got to play with him. My mom brought me breakfast and lunch and then made me dinner. A few of my cousins dropped by to say "hi", and then Shawn's aunt Lisa came over to see us as well. She brought me some new pants and about four meals to keep in the freezer for when we need dinner. Also, Lexi got a gift and some brownies!

After everyone left and Lexi was tucked into bed, I was able to get on the computer and read some of the comments people have sent to me. I am just overwhelmed by the amount of people that are willing to help us. Customers from mine and my husband's work and friends of the family we haven't seen in years. Even people from all over the WORLD that I have never even met are sending me words of encouragement and helping in any way that they can. I haven't been able to stop smiling for the last few hours.

Tomorrow morning I have a doctor's appointment at 9am. I think it is just for a count check and I'm hoping we will have some information on the bone marrow donor search too. I'm not certain that I am out of the woods on needing a transfusion, so I guess that is always a possibility. I hope not though, sitting in the clinic all day isn't my idea of a good time.

I'm not a real big "shout-out" type person because I don't want to feel like I am leaving one person out when I thank another, but sometimes it's called for. I really, really want to thank Rob Jones, who is an amazing long time friend of my family. He has built a website for me and has been spreading the word like crazy in order to gather support for me. He and some friends of his, Sheldon (Doc) and Cricket, are really working hard to let everyone know what we are going through. The Internet can be a truly amazing thing and I am in tears as I write this thinking about all the new friends that are following my story. All of you who feel inspired by me, know that each and everyone one of you, be it my grandmother, my brother, my co-workers, or anyone who stumbled upon my blog by any means, you all keep me going. You all make me smile and feel that the world isn't anywhere as near of a terrible place as some people think.

Thank You, everyone!

Posted by Rachel at 9:37 PM

Thursday, July 29, 2010

Hurry up and wait

I guess we are playing the hurry up and wait game right now. I went to the doctor this morning and everything still looks fine. My blood counts are good and steadily climbing, but they aren't high enough to do the biopsy. I will go back on Monday and have them recheck and assess the situation again. We will continue to do that every couple days until they are where they need to be. I don't exactly know where they need to be, but I suppose as long as someone at my doctor's office has an idea, I don't really care. Right now I am enjoying the fact that I feel well and can do "most" anything I want, from inside my house with limited visitation that is.

The doctor I spoke to today made me feel a lot better about the transplant, better than anyone has really. He was the first person to look at me and basically say, "Look you've been through a lot, you've had chemo and you've been sick. We give you a lot of chemo all at once. Yes, you will get really, really sick but it's for like a week or two. The rest of it is just incredibly boring; a lot of sitting in the house, or sitting in the hospital NOT getting sick". It was nice to have someone say, relax it's bad, but probably not as bad as you're thinking.

After the doctor, I talked my mom into letting me go to one store real quick since it was 9 am and probably pretty clear of people. We stopped at Old Navy because Lexi wanted a shirt to match Mommy today. We couldn't find an exact match but we got close enough, so she was happy.

Posted by Rachel at 2:00 PM

This just in

It actually was "just in" about five hours ago, but I didn't get a chance to update until now. My oncologist's office called and said they have scheduled my bone marrow biopsy for Monday morning. We should know by the end of the day Monday where we go from here.

I'm exhausted. Goodnight!

Posted by Rachel at 10:04 PM

Friday, July 30, 2010

Here come the worry warts!

Well, I know they say that worrying gets you nowhere...but it doesn't seem to help the worry go away. Today is not a great day for me. First of all, I just woke up and it's almost 1pm. I am exhausted because I am not really sleeping much at night. I am fine during the day, but for some reason at night when I lay down is when my mind starts to race. How am I going to afford all the stuff we need? Will Lexi get to school on time everyday without me? What if my husband gets sick, who will take care of him? Are the tellers at work stressed out because they are short handed? My worry is endless; from the smallest of concerns to the biggest problems you could ever face in your life. My biggest battle right now is against worry. I have been reading a lot about transplants, and talking to people on message boards that have been through this and it's always the same answer. One day at a time, you never know what will happen. Yes, I know I could walk outside and be hit by a bus and die, but that doesn't make me feel any better.

I have two issues. First, I am an absolute 100% control freak. Nothing to me is considered "under control" until it is done or I am in control of it. When someone says "relax, we will take care of it," it tends to make me worry more. It makes me realize that I am dependent on someone else to make sure my life functions as it needs to. That is hard. Second, the number one thing I HATE is to be is a burden. If I for one second feel that I am putting someone out in any way, I don't like it. Ask my husband. I am not even good at picking a place to eat just in case he doesn't like the place I pick. I am absolutely a people pleaser. I was born that way. What I am facing right now is the exact opposite. There is almost nothing in my life right now that I am not dependent on other people for. I can't cook for myself, I can't go to the store for myself, I can't work for myself, I am pretty dam helpless in a lot of ways. It's only going to get worse for a while, too.
Uh, don't worry too much. I will snap out of this soon enough. I just had

to put it out there. We are all friends around here anyway, right?

Posted by Rachel at 12:41 PM

Saturday, July 31, 2010

I forgot I was sick.

I was able to spend most of my day thinking about things not related to Cancer. That, my friends, is a success. That was mostly possible because today was a rather eventful day, or at least it was after I woke up at noon. I couldn't fall asleep again last night so finally around three in the morning I took some medicine to help me sleep, which not only knocked me out, but it kept me out for a while. After I woke up, my mother-in-law, grandmother-in-law and my niece, Kyleigh, came to see me. My birthday is on Wednesday so they brought me lots of gifts, mostly different things for my new office downstairs and comfortable clothes for me to wear while I am going through all the fun. Then, my older brother came over and we went to the store. I didn't buy anything but it was nice to be out of the house. By the time we got home my husband had already left for the benefit (more on that later) so my brother hung out with me for a little while before he headed back home. Then my sister-in-law came over with three of her kids, my adorable twin nephews and my other new niece, Abby. While she was here, my husband got back home and my mother-in-law stopped by again, this time with my step-father-in-law. Then everyone went home, my husband started watching the Rangers game, and I came to update all of you on my day.

Told you my day was eventful! I am at an in-between time where I am healthy enough to see a few people, but once I go for my biopsy on Monday we have no idea when I will be back in the hospital. If I don't see them now, it might be a while.

So, back to the benefit thing. My family put together a benefit dinner for me at a local restaurant that is actually owned by my Aunt Claire and new Uncle Brian. (For those of you following along, they were the ones who got married and I was supposed to be in the wedding, but couldn't go) I wish I could have been there, but I guess if I was healthy enough to be AT the benefit I might not NEED a benefit, right? ;) I am just very thankful to everyone that is working so hard to help me out all over the town, and literally all over the world.

Anyway, that's enough for tonight. My Grammy is supposed to come see me tomorrow morning so I better try and get to bed early tonight.

Goodnight Friends!   <3

Posted by Rachel at 9:51 PM

Sunday, August 1, 2010

Don't worry, about a thing...

'Cause every little thing is gonna be alright! Sorry, I have that Bob Marley song stuck in my head.

So tomorrow is the day of my follow-up biopsy. I thought I would be really nervous about it, but I'm not. I just seem to have this 'whatever' attitude about all of this right now. It's nice and I hope it lasts. Not being stressed is a good thing. It's helped out a lot the past few days. I've been able to get out of the house a couple of times and I've seen quite a bit of my family.

Speaking of family, some of my family came over to celebrate my birthday with me. Since I might be in the hospital on my actual birthday, they decided to come over today. Dad made steak and crab legs (my favorite), and we watched the video of my aunt's wedding. My brother made me a cake, too. My Grammy wasn't able to come see me, but she did send a gift for me with my Aunt Barbara and cousin, Christiana. It was really strange because I woke up this morning thinking about how I would love to get a locket necklace before I went in for transplant; one that I could wear with a picture of my daughter in it. It turns out that one of the gifts my Grammy got me was a silver locket that says "Peace Be With You" on the front. I was so happy. I have a sneaking suspicion my Poppy snuck into my dream and whispered it to me while I was sleeping last night.

I guess I better get to bed since I have to be at the hospital very, very early tomorrow. I will make sure I update everyone as soon as I know something, good, bad or indifferent.

Posted by Rachel at 10:26 PM

Monday, August 2, 2010

Marrow Donor

I spoke to the transplant coordinator at my hospital a little bit ago and she had good news. It looks like the results of my donor search are in. We have SEVERAL preliminary options for a perfect donor match. She has put in a request to contact two of the donors, one on the domestic registry and one on the international registry. She said even if neither one of those work out, not to worry because there are plenty more matches.

All I can say is GOD is good!

I will update again once we have biopsy results...

Posted by Rachel at 11:41 AM

Update for the day, Part 2

As I updated all of you earlier, we did find out that we have quite a few preliminary matches for a bone marrow donor. What that means is there are several people that have the likelihood of being a perfect match if they pass their next round of testing. They will have a more in depth DNA testing done, and also testing to ensure they don't have one of several viruses/diseases that are known to complicate the transplant process. I cannot stress enough how lucky I am to have this many options for a match. Most people are lucky if they find one partial match option. It is because there are so many wonderful people around the world that have joined the registry that I have this opportunity. PLEASE, let this encourage all of you to consider joining the National Marrow Donor Program if you can.

The second part of my day, as you all know, was receiving the results of my bone marrow biopsy that I had early this morning. Unfortunately, the chemo I had last week was not enough to get me where I need to be for transplant. This means that I will be receiving another round of chemotherapy starting on Wednesday morning. It will be a several hour infusion for five days in a row. It's a stronger chemotherapy than anything I've ever had and I anticipate being very ill for several weeks from it. My doctor has told me this medication is considered a bridge to the transplant, meaning it is only given to patients who are preparing to go into a transplant. I have to admit that I am very nervous about this because they did refer to this chemotherapy as "the big guns" and that just doesn't sound fun. I am just trying not to think about it. Today went well, we got some good news and we got some bad news, but overall I am okay today. That is all I can ask for.

Posted by Rachel at 9:13 PM

Tuesday, August 3, 2010

If tomorrow never comes

So far today I am not feeling well at all. I think it is a mix between my procedure that I had yesterday and anxiety about tomorrow and what the next week will bring me. I am sort of just taking it easy and letting my husband take care of everything. I am stuck in my room for a while I'm afraid. I started getting dizzy trying to go up and down the stairs earlier, so that means I have to pick which half of the house I want to stay in. Usually the half with my bed in it wins! My mom had mentioned trying to replace the couch in my office downstairs with a day bed so that when I got tired I didn't have to hike up the stairs. I wasn't too sure that was necessary, but today it is sounding like a pretty good idea.

I feel like today is rushing by. I would really like time to stand still for a while. I don't want to deal with tomorrow, so if it doesn't come, I don't have to, right? Of course there is part of me that is anxious for the next three weeks to fly by so we can have this behind us, find out that it worked, and get to a transplant. If you don't start, you can never finish!

Posted by Rachel at 1:13 PM

50

Wednesday, August 4, 2010

What a difference a day makes.

As you all know I was really dreading my visit to the clinic this morning. I was having a lot of anxiety about the new, very intense chemotherapy my oncologist had decided I needed. Besides the fun of that, today is my 24th birthday so I was bummed about having to spend my birthday sick in the hospital.

When I arrived at the clinic my doctor had a few things he wanted to talk to me about. First, he felt another day delay wouldn't hurt anything and he wanted me to take the day to celebrate my birthday and not be stuck in the hospital getting medicine.

Second, and most importantly was after he reviewed my treatment history again and had some time to do more research, he has elected to not give me the Clofarabine (that's the name of the super scary/strong stuff). He has instead elected to give me a four-week course of four different medicines. This combination is one that I have had twice before but not quite as strong as I will get this time. We know that this regimen is hard on me, very hard on me. With that being said, my husband and I both agree that maybe it is because it works so well. It has induced remission for me two times before so we are hoping that it will work just one more time. The point of changing up the treatment regimen is because my doctor is unsure that my leukemia is truly refractory, or chemo resistant, and he does not want to give me a medication with very serious possible side effects until we have exhausted all of our other options. I tend to agree with him. We will do another biopsy in three weeks to make sure that this is working and that we don't need to move on to the Clofarabine.

The most amazing part to me is that I had a dream last night. It was just one of those dreams where nothing really happens; you just hear a voice telling you something. In my sleep I just heard this voice asking me why my doctor won't try what worked before, why he doesn't give that another shot. I hadn't even had a chance to discuss that dream with my husband, but I planned to mention it to my oncologist, Dr. Bowman, just because. I assumed that it was probably just my mind wondering as it sometimes does. When my doctor walked into the room this morning and starting telling me his plan I knew GOD was trying to tell me something. He is leading me to my cure, one step at a time. I can feel it today more than ever.

Posted by Rachel at 3:42 PM

Thursday, August 5, 2010

Round 2, Day 1

Today was my first round of chemo on our second attempt at getting me into remission. This is the layout for my next 4 weeks:

The first day of week one (today), I received intrathecal chemotherapy. Intrathecal means into the spinal fluid, and if you know anything about spinal fluid, you know the only way to get medicine into it is with a spinal tap. No big deal though, I've done it so many times that I am used to it. Dr. Bowman does them really quick and it's over in no time. The only problem I had today was with one of the meds they gave me called Ativan, a strong anxiety medication given so that I basically don't give a rip about the whole procedure. It makes me very nauseous if they push it through my line too fast. Well, they pushed it too fast and I threw up A LOT right before my procedure, and that made me feel bad for a while.

I will also receive a combination of three other chemo's, once a week for the next four weeks. Two of which I got today, and one I will get tomorrow. After tomorrow, I should only have to visit the clinic once weekly for the next month. The chemo's are Vincristine, L-Asparaginase and Daunorubicin. I don't really know the "by the book" side effects of these drugs, but I can tell you my experience of what they do.

Vincristine - Well, Vincristine and I do NOT get along very well at all. She makes my hands go numb, my feet get really heavy causing me to have trouble walking, and I get a great deal of bone pain. Not to mention she gives me heartburn, ugh. Oh, and she is the reason I've been bald for two years. If only I could run into her in a back alley somewhere ...

L-Asparaginase- I call this one "Leg-Shot," simply because that's what it is. Two nurses come in with giant needles and inject this chemo into my thighs. Fun, huh? This medicine, though somewhat painful to receive, doesn't have too many side effects. Obviously my muscles are sore for a few days, but that isn't anything that little snot Vincristine wouldn't have done anyway.

Daunorubicin - Dauno for short, is just your typical pain in the ass chemotherapy. Makes my heart race, makes me throw up a lot, get over heated easily, and turns my pee dark red. Nothing special - just sucks.

Isn't this fun, we are learning so much today!

Now the only other medication I am taking is a daily steroid, a rather high dose of Prednisone. I have to take 30mg three times a day for four weeks. Let's say this about Prednisone; if I were Superman, this would be my Kryptonite. The first day or two I will be okay, but then I will start out with heartburn that feels like Hell is literally located in my stomach (partly because this is taken with Vincristine and they are like a tag team of death!) Nothing will help. I have tried every combination of heartburn medication out there. I have eaten licorice, ginger in every form you can think of, changed my diet more than 1000 times (I wish I was exaggerating), etc. The best part is that the heartburn and other stomach problems from this medication make it miserable when I eat, which is fun all in itself. Add in the fact that the main side effect of this medication is an increase in appetite, and it's doubly fun. I could eat enough to feed two grown men a day easily while I am taking this. How incredibly unfair is that? Anyway, other fun stuff this steroid has done for me is given me severe anxiety to the point that I have panic attacks just from leaving the house. It causes me to hallucinate (yup, that's right - I see crap that isn't there, and it's weird)! I have deep bone and muscle pain and I swell up like a chipmunk. Literally in about a week my face will look like I am storing nuts for a long cold winter. I'll have to take a picture...it's kind of funny...for you guys at least. ;)

I am sure I will have bad days but hopefully I can still find some humor in all of this. Thankfully I have a husband that will be with me no matter what. If I want to laugh at my chipmunk face, he will laugh with me but still tell me that I am the sexiest woman alive. If I want to cry, he will bring the tissues and let me cry all night in his arms if that is what I need that day. If I wanna be pissed off, we can bitch for hours about anything and everything Cancer related. Sometimes it's pointless, but hey, it makes me feel better!

Sorry this was so long, but I know that the next few weeks will bring a lot of ups and downs in my day-to-day feelings, both mentally and physically. The more I can let you all in on what's going on, the better you can understand.

Goodnight Friends!

Posted by Rachel at 9:04 PM

Friday, August 6, 2010

Cancer Rules!

"I wish I had Cancer, 'cause that means I would get cute band-aids"
– Lexi

Isn't it amazing some of the things kids will say? I have to say though, hearing things like that from my little girl makes me smile. It helps me to realize that we as a family are doing a great job of making sure the little Princess is not scared of what Mommy is going through, as she shouldn't be. I am sick, but there is nothing for her to be afraid of. All she needs to know is that I get cool band-aids and she gets extra time with Grandma and Papa. Cancer Rules!)

I got my "Leg-shots" at the clinic earlier today. That was great fun. They surprised me with an extra one for good measure. I guess when you're a VIP patient you get bonus prizes from time to time. Oh well, I will take ten leg shots if that is what Dr. Bowman thinks it will take to get this crap under control. It's okay though; it hurts but not as bad as you might think. Do you want to know one of the many advantages of seeing a Pediatric Oncologist? Numbing cream! They give me a cream that numbs the skin so I only feel it once it gets into the muscle and the medicine starts going in. (Did I mention this blog isn't for the squeamish? If I've gotta do it, you can read about it. LOL)

After we hung out for about an hour at the clinic to make sure I didn't have a reaction to the medication, we got to come home. Lexi got here shortly after we did and now she and Shawn are at the grocery store. As for me, I intend to take a VERY LONG nap after I finish telling all of you about my lovely day.

Oh and my Uncle Ernie made me some chicbvbbbbvken noodle soup today. I am having a hard time keeping anything but soup down, and Campbell's doesn't cut it like it used to.

Not too much exciting to write about today; which is a good thing. If you find yourself yearning for more of my clever writings, I invite you to re-read some of the past posts, because this is all I got! ;)

Posted by Rachel at 4:55 PM

Saturday, August 7, 2010

It's like the flu, but better.

My day today pretty much consisted of a whole lot of nothing. I woke up earlier than I hoped, mostly because I was so uncomfortable. I didn't sleep much last night to begin with, but I woke up with a sore throat and an ear ache. If that wasn't enough I was burning up and freezing cold all at the same time, pretty much non-stop since the middle of the night. Kind of like when you have the flu except for me this will last for about 3 1/2 more weeks and get worse each day; one of the many things the steroid is good for. My husband did pull out one of his trusty Under Armour shirts for me to wear, which has helped some. I am still cold/hot but it at least keeps me from sweating so much.

My mom came over this morning to get Lexi and take her to get fitted for her cheerleading uniform, she brought me some Chloraseptic spray, too. Then, I think she did like six or seven hours of running around for me while working on several different fundraisers she has going on. Now I think she is about to crash and burn from exhaustion. You gotta love her. Lexi gets to spend the night at Grandma and Papa's tonight, which I know she is excited about. Mom said she is curled up in bed watching a movie with my dad. She is a princess like that. I have to say I am truly thankful for my parents and I don't know what I would do without them. We are going on nine years with this Cancer crap and they are still there for me like I was diagnosed yesterday. They pretty much dedicate all of their free time (which isn't much to start with) to me in making sure I have whatever I want. I think I can safely say that I have the best parents in the world.

Anyway, I am coming up on my ten o'clock meds. I am going to try and take something to help me sleep so I can pass out before I get too uncomfortable. Wish me luck on sleeping more than 5 hours tonight. I need it!

Oh – I almost forgot, the dog and I both took a bath today (not together). That's cool, right?)

10 o'clock meds – just because my day was that fun.

Posted by Rachel at 9:29 PM

Sunday, August 8, 2010

Maybe I should have slept a little longer.

Well, the sleeping medicine worked. I slept from about 1am until 12pm and I only woke up once through the night. It took me an hour to fall back asleep, but that is much better than I've been doing. I woke up with a terrible stomachache so I took a little bit of everything I had to help with that; then I ate some eggs that my husband made for me. That helped...for about an hour. Then I pretty much set up shop on the floor of the bathroom with my iPod until I had cleared everything out of my stomach that I had eaten in the past 3.5 years. Or at least that's what it seemed like. I feel a little better now as I am slowly introducing my stomach to some ginger ale. We will stay away from the medicine for a little while. My body doesn't seem to want that at the moment. At least just the optional stuff that is, can't avoid all of it, right?

Some of my family and friends are at another fundraiser for me today. I don't know much about it, and I guess I don't really need to. I will just do what I always do...smile and feel absolutely grateful for every penny that they collected when they get done.

My husband is going back to work tomorrow and though I am not crazy about it, we gotta do what we gotta do. Since the switch up in my treatment has put my transplant off by approximately seven weeks, we obviously can't afford for him to stay away from work that long. He is going to work about three days a week for now and then stay home with me on the days I go to the doctor, and whenever we expect I'll feel the worst. My mom will likely be here most of the time when he is gone, which is nice. She will cook me whatever I want, and she is always cleaning or planning something while she is here. Plus, Lexi can be home with all of her toys and I can see her during the day more. That is until she starts school in a little over a week. (I can't believe I am even saying that, it still seems unreal!)

Anyway, I hope everyone has a great Sunday. Looks like it is a beautiful but hot day outside!

Hugs,

Rachel

Posted by Rachel at 3:16 PM

Monday, August 9, 2010

What a LONG day!

Wow! Today was a very long day. Well, I suppose it wasn't any longer of a day then yesterday, but it felt like it. I got up kind of early to go visit Lexi's school. Got a lot of questions answered and I think we are all ready for Kindergarten when it starts soon. Well, maybe a few more school supplies and another dress or two, but you get the point. After my mom and I got back from the school she did some grocery shopping for me since this steroid is causing me to eat us out of house and home. Lexi and I just laid around and watched TV in bed for a few hours and then took a nap until my husband got home from work. He made us dinner, and then my mom came back by with my niece for a little while. Love that little squirt. Oh, and her brother too!

My heartburn is starting to get really bad today, which is never pleasant for me. That is one of the worst side effects I get with my chemo/steroid combo. I have been able to battle it for a few days without much trouble, but my dose is so high I knew it wouldn't last long. B. Prevacid 2x daily may say it is optional on the bottle, but it is non-negotiable!

I think tomorrow my dad is going to come spend some time with me, and Mom is going to do some more grocery shopping. She is like a thrift queen when it comes to buying groceries, but it requires careful planning and visits to several different stores to get the best deals. So I guess she is gonna finish up her "adventures in grocery shopping" in the morning.

In other random news, I think I have a leaky faucet. No not in my plumbing anywhere, but in my nose. I tend to forget how terrible my allergies are when I don't leave the house. I left for an hour this morning to go to the school and I think I've gone through an entire box of Kleenex since I got home!

With that I hope everyone had a good day today, and has an even more fantastic one tomorrow I am going to head off to bed and hope for the same for me.

G'night!

Posted by Rachel at 9:54 PM

Tuesday, August 10, 2010

In summary

My face feels like it is on fire.
My stomach hurts.
My nose won't stop running.
I can't remember if I took my allergy medicine or not.
I am hungry, but I don't feel like eating.
My T.V. isn't working.
My heart won't stop racing, so I have to just stay in bed.
I want to take a bath.
My daughter is getting sick - she has a fever.
I am sick of depending on everyone, for everything.
I want to drive my car.
I want some tea, but I know that won't go well.
I don't want to go to the doctor on Friday.
I wish I was at work.
I wish Shawn was home.
I can't sleep.
I don't want to take my medicine.

Today sucks.

Posted by Rachel at 3:57 PM

Wednesday, August 11, 2010

7 down, 21 to go.

If anyone is curious of how long it takes 90mg/day of Prednisone to completely start kicking your butt, the answer is seven days. In the past 24 hours I have managed to completely swear off the entire White Castle franchise because of what their little burgers did to my stomach in terms of heartburn. I think my husband may have received 1-3 additional buttholes last night after I yelled at him for treating me like a child. I fell asleep just as the sun was coming up this morning, and proceeded to sleep on and off for about 20-30 minutes at a time throughout the rest of the day today. Then I called my mom as soon as I woke up and starting crying because she hadn't been to the grocery store for me yet. I wasn't even hungry. I just wanted her to go because I can't.

I unfortunately don't think that any of this would have happened if I had any control of my emotions. What can you do? Sorry guys...

I also have decided I am going to start searching E-bay for one of those Men-in-Black-esque mind erasers. I think it could really come in handy for me during my treatment. I am at the point where I am old enough that I have to consent to my own treatment. What that means is I get to sit there and listen to a long speech from my doctor about everything that could go wrong with the medicine they are about to give me. I have to then sign the consent for it, watch them give me the medication, and go home and wait for all of the wonderful things to go wrong that sometimes never do. I will then come home and sometimes proceed to search to the ends of the Internet to find every rarity on everything related to my treatment. This helps me to prepare sometimes for what is to come, more and more recently it just induces anxiety that I don't need. Enter mind eraser. I can see it now,   Flash   , "Ouch! My stomach hurts, wonder what that's from? Oh well. Goodnight! By the way honey, where is all my hair?") Hey, a girl can dream, right?

Anyway, hopefully tonight will go a lot smoother and I can sleep a little longer. Medicine induced bliss or not, something has to give.

Posted by Rachel at 6:01 PM

Thursday, August 12, 2010

So far, so good.

I have to say that at least thus far, today has been a pretty good day. I got sick this morning when I woke up, but pretty much smooth sailing from then on. My husband is home with me until Monday, which is great all in itself. He has been working on various things throughout the house and getting some junk done that has been stressing him out. A stress-free husband is always a plus. I have a daybed for my office now; that was given to me. He is working on putting that together too. My brother just left, he made us some lemon chicken for dinner, and now I am just relaxing on the couch watching TV and well, doing this of course. Usually the day before I go to the hospital for an infusion, I can count on it being my best day. It is the farthest point from my last dose of chemotherapy, so I am going to enjoy today and hope for the best after tomorrow's doctor appointment. No sense in thinking anymore about it than that, at least no point that I can see.

I took a trip outside today to visit my mailbox. I don't know if anyone has realized this, but man it's HOT outside! I think I will stick to the inside of my cool house, except for mandatory outdoors trips. That seems to keep me at a safe distance from fainting, and I like that. I wonder if I can sweet-talk my doctor into seeing me somewhere between 10 pm and 3 am for my next week appointment!

<3

Posted by Rachel at 5:46 PM

Friday, August 13, 2010

Some days are worth just skipping right through...

Let me first start off by apologizing for having a short - to the point post.

I am not feeling very well today, and there isn't much to say from there. The doctor appointment went as expected. I got sick and sleepy. I came home, took a nap, and now I am hoping to not throw up anymore since I can't have anymore nausea medicine for a while. I don't know how much of them actually stay in my stomach. The plan for the evening is to lay in bed and consume whatever "easy on the stomach" food I can tolerate until it's bedtime, take my evening medicine and an Ambien, and try this whole thing over again tomorrow.

I figure one of two things can happen. I will either wake up to find that tomorrow is slightly better than today, or that today wasn't quite as bad as I thought. I'll let you know when I get there.

<3

Posted by Rachel at 7:07 PM

72

Saturday, August 14, 2010

A little improvement

I guess in overall terms, today has been better than yesterday. I slept pretty late thanks to my new sleeping medicine, which I am very thankful for. I also have been able to hold down food better, but I am also watching what I eat a little more carefully. I have pretty much spent the day laying around, watching TV, and watching to make sure the wall doesn't fall down in my living room.

My husband is sick today, which makes things difficult. He has been sleeping for a few hours and I hope when he wakes up he will feel better. I don't like being sick, but I really don't like him being sick. I may get to try out the new daybed tonight if he still has a fever when his nap is over.

Tomorrow is a new day though, and I'm sure it will be even better than yesterday and today. I think my Grammy is going to come see me, so that makes me happy. I don't get lots of visitors, so seeing anyone is exciting, but I especially love to see her. My dad is usually off on Sundays too, so he will mostly likely stop by.

Well I guess that about covers it...and even if it doesn't, my laptop is going to die soon so it will have to work.

Until tomorrow... <3

Posted by Rachel at 6:03 PM

One more thing for today...

I've been pretty bummed and lonely the past few days, so I decided it would be a good idea if my husband and I went "out" to eat. I set the back patio table while he went to pick up our to-go order. I am feeling much better. :)

Posted by Rachel at 10:07 PM

Sunday, August 15, 2010

Exhaustion

Wow! I've had a busy day today. Well, as busy a day as I can have I would suppose. First off I woke up earlier than I had planned because my leg is starting to really ache, making it hard to sleep for very long (might be time to try some pain medicine tonight). Then, my Grammy came over to see me for a little while and brought my aunt with her. She also brought me some of my favorite banana pudding ever. My mom came while they were here to visit with me for a little while, too. After they all left I was pretty well exhausted, so I laid down for a nap with the dog while Shawn went to the grocery store. Once he got home we ate a little bit and then went over to my brother's house. It was nice to get out of the house for about an hour and see some family, but I forget how easy it is for me to get completely worn out. Sitting at a table and walking around a house even in the smallest doses makes me feel like I ran a marathon all day long. Plus, my anxiety gets really bad when I am away from home because I am away from the things I know. Be it my pillow, my bathroom, a medicine, whatever. Routine and comfort are two very big parts of this, and I tend to take that for granted. I guess you could say that sometimes being stuck at home in isolation is a blessing in disguise.

My princess is home and that makes me happy, but since it is 8:30 and her bath is almost over I better start making my way upstairs. Bedtime doesn't go smoothly without a bedtime story from Mommy.

Posted by Rachel at 8:19 PM

Monday, August 16, 2010

What's your purpose today?

As the days go by and they become more physically and emotionally demanding on me, I spend a lot of time contemplating purpose, the purpose of a lot of things. You see, if I didn't have an absolute purpose for everything I do everyday, there would be no reason to go through all of this. If I didn't see a reason to want to hold on to my life so dearly, well then I would have been handed a golden ticket. If I were to do nothing at all about my health from this point forward, I wouldn't have to deal with anything ever again. Luckily though, in all my soul searching I have actually begun to find MORE purpose in my life. That is a good thing, in my opinion.

Not that I would wish this upon anyone, but there are many people in my own life that I wish I could share this experience with, if only in part. The part that makes you appreciate your body and your life in general. The part where you watch yourself in a mirror fade away over the course of a few weeks. The part that makes me want to scream at everyone and say, REALLY? You want to go out and get wasted tonight, take drugs, and ruin the only body you will ever have, for fun? (If you can even call it that) Now don't worry, I'm not going to get on my high horse and act like I am better than anyone and that I am only going to put the healthiest things into my body from here on out, but I can tell you that I am painfully aware right now how easily you can lose it. Physically, emotionally, whatever it may be, take care of your life. You can't expect anyone else to do it for you.

If you're not happy with your life, change it...because you can. Change it to have a purpose. Don't just spend your every day surviving until the next time the sun comes up. Surviving is what you do because you have to, and it is most definitely not a way of life. I am surviving Cancer, yes – but life, I am living.

Posted by Rachel at 3:45 PM

Tuesday, August 17, 2010

Tidbits of fun for your day.

My day today has pretty much been consumed with piddly stuff that lead up to a lot of nothing except for the fact that another day is almost over, and we are close to the half way point in this phase of treatment. It is a four-week phase and two weeks will be up on Thursday. That's pretty cool.

I haven't been getting around much today because my legs are really starting to ache. My doctor did suggest that I try to walk around some each day just to maintain what strength I can, so I am doing a little. Don't worry though, if all I do in a given day is walk to the bathroom and back, I think I am getting PLENTY of exercise, sheesh. I just have to keep the balance between "am I strong enough to walk around?" and "am I going to faint trying to get over there?" Fainting sounds painful, we won't push that one. I am sure my lovely medical team would agree with the logic behind that.

I woke up early this morning at like 6am, but THANK GOD I was able to fall back asleep. Would you believe I slept until ten? I woke up and thought I had won the lottery. I think I was only awake for about three hours in the middle of the night, too. Everyone has goals; sleeping more is mine. Oh, and to be able to go to the new Olive Garden by our house so I can gorge myself on all you can eat soup, salad and breadsticks. It's just a rip-off when you get it to go...

Posted by Rachel at 7:43 PM

Thursday, August 19, 2010

Just checking in.

Here's just a quick note to apologize for not updating the past few days. I'm just kind of in a funk right now. I am sure you all understand. I'll snap out of it soon enough I'm sure. I see the doctor in the morning, so I'll at least let you know how that goes. Thanks for bearing with me.)

Posted by Rachel at 10:34 PM

Saturday, August 21, 2010

See, I'm still here. Somewhere.

Okay, so I'm sorry to leave everyone hanging for the past few days, but don't worry - I am still here. I've been a little taxed physically and mentally both, so I took some time to sleep, stare at the wall, and update Facebook just enough to let everyone know I was still around.

My doctor's appointment yesterday went well. I slept almost the entire time I was there and I just remember them waking me up to say it was time to go home. That was quite pleasant actually. Came home, took another long nap and then took my little girl to "meet the teacher" night at her school. She is so excited to start, and I am excited for her. I know she is going to love it.

I am having a hard time right now finding a balance between foods that fill me up and foods that don't upset my stomach. I know that doesn't seem like a big struggle, but I have lost almost nine pounds in the last month and I didn't have it to give up. Chicken nuggets and Easy Mac may settle well with my medicine, but they don't give me a lot of strength. My poor husband, GOD love him, does his best but he hasn't been bitten by the cooking bug and I don't expect that he will. I can only handle so many frozen "insert random Stouffer's entree here" items.

One more week until my next biopsy to see where we go from here. No more updates from the transplant team, but I am not thinking about that much. I am doing well enough handling all of this one day at a time and having no expectations. As long as that keeps working, I'll go with it.

Posted by Rachel at 5:22 PM

84

Monday, August 23, 2010

What just happened?

I am not exactly sure that I can break down for you what has happened in the last few days, but man oh man, it feels like I have been on a whirlwind. Lexi started her first day of school today, which means any ounce of energy I've had in the past four days has been dedicated to that (which isn't much to begin with) and I am exhausted. I came home to a three-hour nap as soon as we dropped her off, but it was so worth it. Even if it lands me in the hospital for a month of Sunday's, (as my Grammy would say) I would do it all over again. Thanks to the frantic shopping and gathering efforts of her grandparents and my amazing husband, I was able to have the picture perfect first day of school for my little girl that I've been planning since the day I found out I was pregnant. I got to make her a super special lunch and snack and we laughed in bed last night about all the wonderful things she was in for today, we even made up a new song. We re-did "Mary had a Little Lamb" into a song about our little white fluffy dog, Corbin. We call it, "Lexi has a Little Dog!"

This morning came early but I was ready. I even stood outside her bedroom door with the video camera while I waited for her alarm to go off. Grandma came over to cook us a big breakfast and Papa got to sit down and eat with all of us before he had to head off to work. The outfit she picked out for today, matching earrings and necklace, her perfectly curly locks, and all the pictures and video you can imagine, all turned out just as I hoped. We got to the school and we walked her to the classroom just like every other Mommy and Daddy taking their baby to their first day of school. We left the Cancer, and the chemo and the panic attacks at home, and I was just Mommy. She even joked as we were walking into the school about how her lunch box was too heavy because Mommy over packed it. Mission Accomplished.)

For my spirit, there is nothing I can imagine that would be better than how I feel right now. Physically, yeah I'm a mess, but I don't care. When I first found out about my transplant one of my first reactions was that I could never have imagined missing my baby's first day of school. Then I thought, well maybe if I can at least be at home I can see some of the good stuff. Guess what Cancer - I win. I was there with all that I had, and it was amazing! GOD is good, ALL the time!

Posted by Rachel at 1:13 PM

Tuesday, August 24, 2010

One more day done.

So we made it through the second day of school and I am spent! I think it all finally hit me today like a ton of bricks. I have been a zombie since the moment I woke up. I got out today to eat lunch and go to Walgreens, and I felt like I took a trip to Thailand and back. Luckily it is just about time for my last medicine of the night and then I am off to sleep. Lexi's lunch is made and clothes are out for tomorrow so my husband told me to not even bother getting up in the morning. He would get her off to school. I will do my best to let that happen; I know I need the rest.

Shawn grilled a good steak and made baked potatoes and garlic bread all by himself tonight for dinner. He even read up on how to marinate it in honey mustard sauce. I was so proud of him. Plus the red meat is good for my strength.

My mouth sores and stomach are really starting to bother me quite a bit now, but I am just trying to deal with each issue as it comes. I'll just rotate the control medicine and sleep through as much as I can. One day at a time we are doing this thing.

Until tomorrow, Goodnight everyone!

Posted by Rachel at 9:21 PM

88

Sunday, August 29, 2010

Makes me tired just thinking about it.

I think I can safely say that the past few days have been the most physically and emotionally taxing days I have had thus far in my treatment.

Friday morning we had the biopsy and my scheduled chemotherapy. Everything from that went really well. The hope was that after three weeks of this regimen the amount of leukemia or "blast cells" in my bone marrow would be around 5%. (They were 30% at relapse and the initial chemo course did not change this number at all, which was alarming.) The biopsy results including the slow growing baby cells in my marrow came out to about 6%. That is good news. It means the treatment is working. I went ahead and received my last round of chemo on this course and I can now start on a lower dose of my steroid for a little while. The plan is to go back to the doctor at the end of this week for a check-up, possibly get a break of chemotherapy for 1-2 weeks and then another dose of something before we head into transplant. We are thinking this will be around three weeks from now.

The REALLY bad part though has been the physical part. Obviously after four weeks of intense chemotherapy and steroids, my body is struggling to hold on. Getting up and walking on my own isn't really an option too much, and my husband has to get me in and out of bed. I am also starting to get some signs of thrush in my mouth so they put me on an antibiotic for that. My stomach might hate that medicine more than anything I have ever had in my life (that combined with the five chemo's and steroid withdrawal, that is). I spent about half the night on Friday lying awake trying to decide how quickly I could "run" to the bathroom, and the other half laying on the floor of the bathroom because I didn't have the strength to go back and forth anymore. Literally being "knock you on your ass" sick all night is one thing, but try doing it while you can barely walk and on a super sleep aid and miserable doesn't come close. Last night was about half as bad. I didn't take the sleeping medicine just so at least getting up would be easier, and I took my medicine a tad earlier. Tonight we're gonna skip the antibiotic all together and try to take it during the day tomorrow. Maybe at the very least I'll get in a nights rest and then start over. If that doesn't work, we will go from there. I have been keeping my husband on his toes trying to think of ways to make this all easier. God Bless him!

It's been taxing, but the doctor did tell me that I shouldn't expect much improvement until next week. Doesn't sound exciting, but I don't feel "behind" when he says that. I'm supposed to be really sick, and I am. It's working. That is what we are looking for, and that is how we don't continue to do this forever.

I am sure I missed a lot as it has been a rough, blurry past few days, but I am going to try and eat, bathe and get some rest while my body will allow it.

Goodnight <3

B. Lexi is a very busy little girl and I am happy she is staying so busy! She had "cheer camp" today for her new cheerleading team, her second week of school starts tomorrow and she goes back to dance class next week. Being her Mommy and keeping her going to all of this stuff keeps us both in great spirits. My baby is such a blessing!)

Posted by Rachel at 9:07 PM

Monday, August 30, 2010

Here's to a brighter tomorrow!

Well, tonight turned into a fail of epic proportion if you ask me. The switching up of the medicine schedule did help me get some more sleep last night, but other than that nothing else went too well. I had two things that I really wanted to do today, one of which was to sit through an hour long Kindergarten orientation in Lexi's classroom at school, and the other was to attend her first cheer practice since I was unable to take her to cheer camp yesterday.

About half way to the school I started getting an ever so intensifying and familiar headache, one that I've had many times before, a spinal headache. They come on fast, strong, and are completely debilitating. The only way to help them is to pretty much instantly lie completely flat. I ignored it as long as I could, but about fifteen minutes into the presentation I had to "run" down the hall to the restroom. When I made it back to the room, the headache and everything else had turned into a full-blown panic attack. It caused me to nearly faint and so I ran back to the restroom and fell on the floor. My husband and I had to leave immediately. Thankfully we live close enough to the school that I was able to make it into the bathroom and then around the corner to my daybed where my legs gave out inches before I could get in it. My husband picked me up, tucked me in, and I've been in this spot ever since.

My mom was already here watching Lexi. She fed her dinner and was getting her ready for practice, so that wasn't much of an issue. Mom is good at the whole cheerleader thing so I am glad she is involved with that. That's the one thing I never did as a kid. Maybe we will talk Grandma into being assistant coach. She doesn't have enough to worry about; ha-ha. Plus, the practice field is almost across the street from their house. I think once things settle down, Lexi will really like the cheerleading. She is already trying to remember the cheers and really wants to see her uniform (I do too. I'm sure I'll have some bows to make.)

Dance also starts in a couple days, but this is our fourth year there and I have no worries about that. They take good care of my kiddo and she likes it there. It's just one more thing to keep the princess happy.

I guess my husband, mother and father have now come to the consensus that I don't get to leave the house anymore for a while, or be left alone for any length of time either. I had a few days where I could feel my legs were weak and gave warning when I needed a rest, but after last night and now several times today, I could walk two steps or two-hundred steps and collapse. No Bueno! It stinks, but I can't argue with them; they are right.

One thing I did forget to mention in yesterday's posts was an update we got on our marrow donors. The original two prospects the coordinator was working on contacting several weeks ago were both contacted. One was an international donor and the other was somewhere here domestically. The domestic donor from what we can gather was too "wishy-washy" and they were never able to set a time for additional testing, but the international donor was located and tested. His results are in and we are just waiting for them to get to us here in the US. It should be any day now from what we were told. When they decided to move on from the flaky domestic donor, they contacted the third match on the list and he went in for his additional testing on Friday. Results should be back on his typing around the first of September, and then a few days after that is when our coordinator will have that information. It seems like they always want to at least compare two when they can, and I am on board with that. Knowing that they have contacted and performed the additional testing on these donors already is a big sigh of relief. It lets us know this may not end up as a never-ending game of phone tag.

Anyway, Lexi asked Grandma to come take her to school tomorrow which is nice because I'm sure my husband won't be doing much sleeping tonight since I can't even roll over well unassisted. As soon as his shower is over I am getting carried up stairs and going to bed. How's that for royal treatment?

Posted by Rachel at 11:11 PM

94

Tuesday, August 31, 2010

All in a day's...something.

Well, so far today has been a better day than yesterday. After realizing my limitations and what it does to me when I push past them, I know to take it easier. My body has enough help trying to give out on me without doing anything myself to make it worse. I am trying to only go up and down the stairs once each day in order to save my energy, but without going insane from sitting in one room all day.

We also cleared some furniture out and made room so I can use the wheelchair in the house. I wasn't thrilled about the idea at first, but after my nasty tumbles over the past few days, it's a much better alternative.

Lexi is starting to open up more about school, so we can see she is actually learning. That is always a good thing. She sang us a song she learned, told us about different parts of a book, and all around had more to say than "I saw Kirby at lunch again today." Kindergarten fits her nicely. She starts dance in two days and then we are officially off and going with all her activities. I like that because that means less meetings, orientations, and lists of things to track down! (I think my mom and husband may appreciate it the most.)

Sorry this post is all over the place today. I am having a hard time writing it. My spinal headache is pretty bad so I have to lay flat and keep a steady stream of Vicodin in me. And as fun as that may sound... Good news on the Antibiotic front, I think my stomach is starting to win! Woo!

Posted by Rachel at 5:14 PM

96

Wednesday, September 1, 2010

Beached Whale

Today I would classify as an all-in-all good day. I still have a terrible spinal headache so I can only get up and move around for a little while at a time, but I think I did as well as I could at managing it. I was able to straighten up my office. (I was driving myself crazy trying to find things!) and that helped. I was also able to help Lexi with her homework while Shawn made dinner, which she wasn't thrilled about doing but she got into it later. (It's an alphabet song, and I had to read to her...can't be THAT bad!) My mother-in-law brought me some big fluffy pillows for my bed so now being stuck in bed all day isn't as bad. Plus, I can't move pillows very well. They have to just be everywhere. I'm like a beached whale at some moments. Ha-ha.

I did have to speak to my doctor today about taking a higher dose of my anxiety medication. I am starting to get much shakier and the slightest thing sends me into a full-blown panic it seems. He agreed that I should take it twice a day and we will revisit the situation when I see him on Friday. Anxiety is one of those things that I never really understood until recently. Even getting help walking to the bathroom can cause extreme panic depending on the way of the wind.

I will just keep working at this like I have been, one day at a time, one problem at a time. Problem? Fix it and move on. It's slightly more manageable that way and keeps me from running to the hills (not that I could literally run anywhere right now ...). I don't know what tomorrow brings, but we will find out when we get there.
I "think" it's Wednesday, so everyone have a great Thursday!

<3

Posted by Rachel at 9:26 PM

Thursday, September 2, 2010

Another good/bad day

What a rollercoaster of a day! First off, I hardly slept at all last night. I think the storms might have had something to do with that. (Don't take that to mean I'm not thankful for the rain.) When I finally got up and moved around a bit, I fell several times. The past few days I could tell when I was gonna give out and needed to sit down, but that isn't the case anymore. If I get up or walk it's gonna have to be with help. Luckily Shawn can get me up and down the stairs when needed and also in and out of the bathtub. It's nice to be married at times like this. Taking a bath could be a lot more awkward.

My parents, siblings and niece and nephew all came over for dinner tonight. I ended up trying to do too much and got panicky and sick, but it was worth it. I really miss seeing everyone. We have a big family, but usually never go more than three days without seeing each other. Hopefully, once I get more and more off this insane steroid I won't have such issues. It's just frustrating really. At least I know that no matter how long this takes it's only temporary and they are family. No one is going anywhere. Well, except my little bro who is leaving for the Navy next week. I can't believe that...

Anyway, doctor appointment in the morning. No chemo on the schedule so it should be uneventful. Maybe we will get some more word on the donor front. You know I'll keep you posted!

Posted by Rachel at 9:52 PM

Friday, September 3, 2010

Friday's Fun

Well, so far today has been a MUCH better day than yesterday. Even though I had a hard time sleeping again last night, my doctor's appointment wasn't very stressful so that really helped my whole day. I was able to get up and help get Lexi off to school and then just relax a little and let my breakfast and morning medicine settle for the trek downtown. We told the doctor about my rough week, but he was confident I should be able to feel much better this coming week. We have a ten day break from chemo and I will be completely off the steroid by Monday. Thank goodness. The one thing they did seem to be concerned with was the amount of weight I've lost recently, so I need to work on putting on some weight from good foods. A week from Monday we will do another bone marrow biopsy and then I will be admitted for a few more days of chemo. It is a five day course, but I may only have to do part of it in-patient. It all depends on how I tolerate it I suppose. I am not getting my hopes up for anything; we will just see how it goes when we get to that point. It will be the same chemo that they referred to as "the big guns" before, but since I am responding better than we originally thought I would to the treatment, it won't be as toxic of a dose and I will just end up with low blood counts and nausea; normal chemo fun.

We asked for an update today on the bone marrow donor situation, but when we left the clinic they didn't have an answer for us. I want to say that they have all of their meetings on Fridays that have to do with the transplant patients. They said we might get an update later today, but since it's already 5:30 pm, I'm thinking not. I'll be worried about it when they give me reason to be, and so far they haven't. What I do know is that our top prospects are both international donors so that makes the whole process take longer at each and every step.

Posted by Rachel at 5:08 PM

Saturday, September 4, 2010

We love Papa!

Thursday evening when my family came over for dinner and I ended the night not feeling so well, Lexi crawled in bed with me while Papa read us both a bedtime story. :)

Posted by Rachel at 12:55 PM

Sunday, September 5, 2010

If this makes any sense.

I am very much out of it today, so this is by ALL MEANS a disclaimer before you read this. Read at your own risk!)

Well, I've made the decision that going through this one full day at a time is way too much to tackle right now. I am now going at it, half day at a time. The mornings seem to be terrible for me since I wake up with no medicine in my system at all, and usually in a lot of pain from lying in one spot for so long. After I get a round of Vicodin, some anxiety medication, and breakfast in me, the day can take a major turn. My biggest problem right now continues to be my strength (or lack of) and my anxiety. It is almost as though the withdrawal from the steroid is worse for my anxiety than the entire time I took it; which isn't surprising, it just isn't fun either and there is no real way to know how long it will last. Increasing my anxiety medication to twice a day has helped me not have mid-day panic attacks, but I just can't get used to this constant medicated feeling. I just lie around most of the day with my head in the clouds and a mild headache. I would describe my emotions lately as a roller coaster, but I'm on too much medication for them to be that all over the place.

Sometimes I want to just be alone in my bed and do nothing but stare off into space. So I do. Sometimes I want to get in the kitchen and cook Thanksgiving dinner, (that is the worst, because I can't even come close to doing that right now). Sometimes I just want my husband to sit next to me and rub my feet (which he does without fail), and then sometimes I wake up and just want my Mommy and Daddy to come cook me over-easy eggs and say hi. (Which, they do too) I am a mess, but I am getting through. By the sheer grace of GOD and lots and lots of love from my family - it's a doable deal!

Posted by Rachel at 3:26 PM

Monday, September 6, 2010

Exhaustion

The word of the day today is EXHAUSTED. I think I woke up more tired this morning than when I went to bed last night. I didn't even know that was possible. I have just had a total lack of energy for some reason. The worst part is I can't seem to nap for the life of me. Today was my last day to take my steroid so hopefully in a few days a lot of this sleep junk will settle down. Once I can sleep I will be able to build some strength back, just in time to go back to the hospital and give it all back! :) Oh well, you take what you can get, right?

I am very proud of myself though. Somehow in my utter exhaustion I managed to make a pretty good dinner for my family. It took me most of the day in several parts to do but it was worth it. I made grilled Teriyaki Salmon and Shrimp with rice. I was in a terrible mood by the time I was through cooking because I was constantly losing my train of thought, but I guess my inner cook went into autopilot and I got it done. It even tasted great! I ate a ton and until that point I had absolutely no appetite all day. (which really helps with the fatigue when you starve yourself of course) My husband said I am a better cook on my worst day than most people are on their best. That made me feel good.

Shawn is going to work a few days this week, so my mom is going to come stay with me. I wish he didn't have to go back to work at all, but unfortunately that isn't the way of the world. We have no idea when this transplant will be and he has to manage his days off the best he can. It will be okay though; I like spending time with my mom. It will be nice to have her here for a few days. With Lexi being in school though, she's probably going to get bored with me. Ha-ha. The house is pretty quiet a lot of the day.

Alright, well Lexi sounds like she is getting out of the bath so that means it's time for Mommy to read a story!

Goodnight everyone! <3

Tuesday, September 7, 2010

Ugh...

I HATE today and I wish it was over.

Posted by Rachel at 6:12 PM

Wednesday, September 8, 2010

Amazing!

So the transplant coordinator from the hospital just called with great news. WE HAVE A CONFIRMED DONOR! All the test results came in and our first choice donor is a perfect match. He is a 28 year-old male. We don't know where he is from, except that he is an international donor.

As soon as my doctor gives the okay, we are ready for the transplant, which means no extra chemo while we wait!

BEST NEWS I'VE HEARD IN A LONG TIME! Praise God!

Posted by Rachel at 12:25 PM

So, what does that mean?

We have a donor - now what? Now that we have a confirmed donor, the next question everyone has is, WHEN IS THE TRANSPLANT?!? Well, we don't know. The donor has been found and tested, and we know when we go to transplant that's where my new marrow will come from, but we don't know much else. As of right now I still have some treatment to go through before I am actually ready for the transplant. The only thing we know for sure is Monday morning I have another bone marrow biopsy and then I will be admitted directly to the hospital for five days of chemo. I have an appointment with the doctor on Friday and we may find out more then, but right now it is sort of a week by week thing. Once I have a biopsy with a low enough percentage of leukemia "blast" cells in it, then we will go for a transplant. Just for numbers sake, at relapse I was at 30%, my last biopsy was 6%, and for the transplant they want to see .01%. We basically will do chemo until we get to there.

Now, having a donor does mean that once we get that .01% we can go straight for the transplant. What we were facing before was that if you don't have a donor but your marrow is ready, you have to get extra chemo to ensure the leukemia cells don't grow back while you're waiting for the transplant. THAT is what's comforting about having a donor right now. I don't want any "extra" chemo.

I hope that clears up a little bit of confusion. I know it's not the best explanation but I tried!)

Posted by Rachel at 9:20 PM

Thursday, September 9, 2010

For the record, I hate coming up with a title.

Today was another rough day for me. I'm starting to get worried that it is so late in the week and I am still not feeling any better. In some ways I am actually getting worse. I was hoping to feel better for at least a few days before I start more chemo and go into the hospital Monday. I still have three days until then, but the outlook is not so good. I do go to the doctor tomorrow morning and fully intend to whine and complain about every last issue I am having. Surely some things can be fixed by changing up some meds and I will get some relief. My number one complaint really is my whole body is in a constant state of numb pain. It's kind of like when your foot falls asleep and then you get up and it starts to hurt as the blood rushes back to it. Well, imagine that all over your body for a week. Pain medicine helps some, but A) I would like to not become addicted to Vicodin so I don't take it around the clock; and B) it seems to be getting progressively worse not better. No bueno. Then of course there is the whole can't really walk, get up, bend over, or hold things because I have no more muscles, problem. My stomach, well we won't even go there. It doesn't even know WHAT is wrong with it. If your stomach has ever done it, mine does it every fifteen minutes. It's like a constant grab bag of different issues. Mouth sores, those suck pretty bad too. Even when my stomach does take a break from being sucky, I still can't really eat much. Good thing I suffered through that antibiotic last week to make sure I didn't get thrush in my mouth. Now my mouth is fantastic (note my sarcasm). A headache for almost two weeks; I get dizzy if I stand up for more than two minutes...

Anyway - I guess I'll stop with the beat down on what makes me feel like crap today. Although, this was a good way for me to lay it out so I know what I am going to tell the doctor tomorrow. Thanks for being my guinea pigs.

Lexi had a very busy day today, and thankfully my mom was able to run her around since Shawn was working. Almost as soon as she got home from school they left to go find her a dress for school pictures tomorrow. I had been putting it off hoping that I would feel well enough to go to the store and look with her, but no such luck. Then she had dance from 5pm-6pm, and cheer practice from 6pm-7pm. She came home, ate dinner, we had some homework to finish, and then the usual bath, story and bedtime. She told me it was the "longest day of my life." She had some moments where she was kind of naughty, but I try to give her some slack because I know she is still adjusting to the long days at school and gets tired pretty easily right now. If I went from doing whatever I want, lying around Grandma's all day to being at school for eight hours a day five days a week, I might be a little bratty, too.

Well, I guess I'm gonna get ready for bed and see if I can be of any assistance to my husband. I know he is tired and would like to get to bed, too. It's been a long week for all of us, and unfortunately next week will be even longer.

Posted by Rachel at 9:06 PM

Friday, September 10, 2010

Not ALWAYS bad.

So I went to the doctor today and guess what happened? They made me feel better!! I told the nurse everything that was going on just like I promised I would, and she actually had some solutions. The first thing she did was put me on some IV fluids. They said I was pretty dehydrated and my mouth was very dry. We were there most of the day for that, but it was worth it. I was also nauseous and in quite a bit of pain when I got there so they switched up my nausea medicine and gave me some morphine. The morphine took away my pain and I was able to sleep for a few hours while I was getting the IV fluids; that was great because I hardly slept at all last night. I woke up pretty hungry so Shawn went and got me a sandwich from Subway. I haven't been able to eat much the past few days so after I finished the whole thing, we knew that was a big step. They sent me home with a different nausea medicine, one I've taken before. Hopefully it will do me some good, just to change it up for a little while. I also got a medicine specifically for nerve pain. That is what's causing my hands and feet to hurt and the dull pain all over my body. It seems like it is pretty strong stuff, but they seem confident it will help. I guess regular pain medicine doesn't do much for nerve pain and that's why I haven't been getting very much relief from what I've been taking. I haven't taken the new pain med yet since I don't start it until bedtime tonight, but the fluids have done wonders already. My mouth hurts, but nowhere near as bad as it did. By tomorrow, I am hoping for even more improvement. I asked for one good day, and I got it. Whatever tomorrow brings, I'll be ready.)

Posted by Rachel at 9:43 PM

Saturday, September 11, 2010

Good day #2

Today was another pretty good day for me, a long day but a good one. Lexi cheered at her first football game this morning and I got to watch the whole thing. It ended up being much hotter than I thought it would be so I didn't dress accordingly and I got pretty hot, but not too bad. I just made sure to drink a LOT of water when I got home and throughout the rest of the day today. I would hate to mess up all the work they did giving me fluids at the clinic yesterday. I had a pretty bad stomachache most of the day, but I think that was more from the Jack-in-the-Box I ate than anything else. I took a nap after we got home and then around dinner time, my in-laws came over to see us. I haven't seen them in a while so it was good to spend time with them. We got dinner from Cheddar's. I ate way too much, we talked for a while and then we showed them the video of Lexi cheering this morning. I'm in bed now, as I don't think I have the energy to do anything but that for the rest of the day. I might try and work up the energy for a shower, but that is even a big maybe. For most people I guess it was a rather uneventful Saturday, but for me, it was a LONG busy day! Thankfully, I am sleeping in tomorrow! :)

Posted by Rachel at 10:13 PM

Sunday, September 12, 2010

Overboard

So tomorrow is the big day. Biopsy first thing in the morning and then we are being admitted. Boo. I've gotten so used to being home that I really don't want to go to the hospital, but it is what it is and it will be over with before I know it. As soon as I know my biopsy results, you know I'll pass along the info.

Since I am starting a new, stronger chemo tomorrow, I can only assume I will be pretty sick and not be able to eat much. Knowing that, I made sure to eat really healthy today. NOT! But I did make sure to eat pretty much everything I have been craving, and I feel dam good about it. Hey, I need to gain some weight anyway. That's my story and I'm sticking to it. I woke up around noon and I was pretty sick to my stomach and still exhausted from the new medicine, (the nerve pain one.) I was worried I was going to be like that all day since this is the first day that I have to take it three times a day. Shawn made me two pieces of toast and lied in bed with me for about a half hour while we laughed at all the noises my stomach was making. After that I started to feel a lot better and was able to eat some more breakfast. I ate some beef taquitos; that was the start to my healthy eating day. Then, my aunt and uncle came to see me and brought me fried rice and orange chicken. It was a little spicy and I was worried it would make me sick, but I did just fine with it and cleaned my bowl. Not one drop of chicken or rice left. Then dinner time came and Shawn and I decided on pizza; pineapple and ham, my favorite. I also have been craving something spicy for WEEKS and decided I was going to go for it. Ten piece hot wings to go with my pizza. I ate them all by myself. Let's just say me and Maalox are hanging out right now. I don't care. Sometimes the stomachache is worth it.

Earlier today I packed Lexi's bag for her week with Grandma and Papa. I know my mom and dad have to think I'm crazy after looking through her suitcase. I wrote a three-page note with detailed instructions for what she had to do each and every day of the week. Which days she was buying lunch, which days they needed to pack her a lunch, which days were gym days, when her library book was due...you name it, it was in the letter. I think I may have told them three times that she needs to take water with her snack. Woops. Then I packed all of her clothes for the week. Each day had its own gallon size zip-lock bag. Inside the bag was each entire outfit complete with socks, shoes, and hair accessories. Most days came with a note giving instructions on everything from how her hair should be to which shoes went where (not every bag was big enough to hold the shoes for its outfit) I also wrote Lexi a note each day for my mom to read to her and stuck them in the bags. Each note wished her a good morning, reminded her to be a good girl and told her something about the day. One day told her it was cheer practice day, another that it was dance day, even one day reminding her she was buying lunch and it was grilled cheese day. I also told her every day to make sure she got a "super stamp" and to call me as soon as school was out. When Lexi looked at the bags on the floor she said, "Mommy, why are there so many notes everywhere!"

I know, I know, my parents are perfectly capable of doing all of those things, WITHOUT the fifteen or so notes I sent along, but what can I say? I have one little girl, she JUST started Kindergarten, and I'm anal. Plus, my hope is that it will make things easier. It's a lot to say "here you go, here's my kid for a week, thanks" even if it is my parents. I want it to be as easy as possible. Open the bag, put the clothes on her, read the card and paper and she is off to school. Plus, they know I'm crazy. I'm sure they half expected something like that! I'm really not worried about it; I am just being overly particular. They know how important Lexi's schedule is to me, and they have only had a MAJOR part in helping me raise her since the day she was born. So it's not like her, or any of this is new to them.

I should probably be in bed by now, but I figure I will make up the sleep tomorrow after my procedure. I'm going to go finish my laundry now. I unfortunately have yet to find any clothes that will fold and *pack themselves.*

Posted by Rachel at 9:57 PM

Monday, September 13, 2010

Good News!!

So far today has been a pretty good day. Well, not physically for me, but the big picture, yes. My procedure went kind of rocky. My husband said when I was knocked out they were pretty rough on me. I was in a lot of pain when I woke up. I required three doses of morphine before I could get comfortable. I've also had a headache all day. I have two doses of Vicodin and I am getting more Morphine now. Hopefully that will take care of this headache. My hips are also killing me where they pulled out the marrow. Again, hopefully this Morphine I'm getting will take care of that. I'd like to not be in pain because they are starting my chemo in about twenty minutes.

Now, on to the good news, my doctor came in a few hours ago to tell us that the preliminary results of my biopsy showed ZERO leukemia cells in my marrow. It isn't "official" until the pathology lab confirms later today, but he looked at it himself. He said he was "very encouraged today." I am so excited. It seems my extra week of feeling bad was because the chemo was working extra hard. Makes it all worth it, for sure!

He also told us that our donor that was found is an 11/11 match to my DNA, which means he is the best possible match we could have found. We knew he was a good match, but we didn't know he was THAT good. Heck, I thought the best we could do was 10/10, apparently it's 11!

Posted by Rachel at 3:33 PM

September 16, 2010

Sorry

Sorry I haven't given an update for a few days but this chemo is much harder than I ever imagined. We are just finishing day 4 of 5 as I type this. The plan is to go home this Saturday and to start what I can imagine will be one hell of a recovery process. Thanks for hangin' in there with me.

Love ya'll!

Posted by Rachel at 10:12 PM

Saturday, September 18, 2010

I made it.

Okay, I made it. I am home! The five day kick-your-ass chemo is over. I have to admit, it was one of the rougher weeks of my life, but we knew it would be bad, and we made it through anyway. Now the "fun" part! I am home, but within the next day or two it sounds like I am going to start getting some pretty major side effects. The pain in my hands and feet are already getting worse, but I've had that happen before. This is just from having so much fluid pumped into me over the last five days. With time, some of that fluid will come out and I will be okay. The big thing is I am going to be VERY susceptible to infection, so home health is coming over this evening to teach Shawn and my mom how to give me IV antibiotic twice a day for four weeks. My port also has to stay accessed the whole time for this, but I am getting used to it. The bad part is taking a shower. I have to wear a giant sticker over the dressing. No fun.

My stomach is pretty much a mess from the antibiotic (which we discussed before, I don't do well with) but the pharmacist gave me some ideas that might help calm it down. Four weeks with a stomach like I had when I was on the thrush medicine is NOT going to cut it. Not to mention I can't take Pepto right now, my only saving grace in all the fun, because it has aspirin in it, which I can't have while on this chemo. Also, I can already tell that I'm going to be extremely exhausted for a while. I slept until 1pm today and I still feel like I could sleep all day long. I got two units of whole blood yesterday and that normally would give me enough energy to run laps for a few days, but not this time. It didn't give me ANY energy at all. That was a bad sign.

I am trying hard to stay ahead of the game on my mouth sores though. Those have gotten pretty bad with my last few rounds of chemo, so I am trying to be one step ahead of them. I know they are going to come whether I like it or not, so I have asked anyone, if they would be willing, to make me any soups, stews, or even easy to eat cold pasta dishes. That way I can eat that now and save my mouth for at least a little while, and then when I do get the mouth sores I can eat more than noodle soup. I can only live off noodles and broth for so long. Anything I can mush up and swallow is going to be my diet for a while. So, any volunteers would be greatly appreciated!

We did get a chance to talk to both my doctor and the transplant coordinator a little more while we were in the hospital. They are thinking it will be about six weeks from now until the transplant. It will take about four weeks for me to recover from the round of chemo I just got, and then we will start the transplant process. I will have a few meetings with the transplant team, tour the transplant unit, have a three or four day full work-up of pretty much everything in my body, and then begin the pre-transplant regimen. We don't know the exact details until the doctors decide and get the results of my tests, but the way it generally works is that I'll get two days of total body irradiation therapy, two days of very high dose chemotherapy, a day of some sort of anti fungal medication, and then however long it takes to get the marrow from the donor to me. I will get the actual transplant either the evening that I get the anti fungal medication or first thing the next morning. Then we pretty much just wait. Wait and deal with side effects as they come along. Generally it takes about five weeks for my new marrow to "en-graft" or take hold of my body and then grow enough for me to be released from the hospital. So IF everything goes according to plan, from what I can figure it will be somewhere around the beginning of December when I will be home from the transplant to start my recovery. How long will it take me to recover from then is really anyone's guess. Usually 100 days from transplant is a big milestone from everything I have read, but that is all I really know. I'm sure one of those fun little meetings I am going to attend will let me know more.

Alright, I've talked everyone's ear off for long enough, so I guess that this is good for now! One more day down... :)
Posted by Rachel at 4:33 PM

Wednesday, September 22, 2010

Terrible, horrible, no good, very bad day(s)

Ever since I got home from the hospital late Friday night, things have kinda' quickly gone downhill. I was experiencing the worst stomach pain I've ever had in my life (and yes, that includes labor)! We tried pretty much anything and everything we could think of to calm it down, at least enough to keep me out of the bathroom for more than ten minutes. Maalox and Mylanta were a joke. I can't take Pepto because it has asprin in it, so who knows on that one. The doctor recommended Immodium, which is a four-hour dose that got me out of the bathroom for a half hour. The fun part was that the whole time I was on the Immodium, I wanted to scream in pain. Finally, Monday morning it was getting worse by the minute, so I told my husband we needed to go to the doctor. After a lot of fluids and Morphine, I have been able to relax. I just can't eat or drink anything for 24 hours and then I'm getting an IV feeding. I am also obviously on round the clock hydration since I was incredibly dehydrated to say the least. There is a virus in my intestinal tract, probably from the chemo spilling into my blood stream, so we are lucky to have caught it early.

They had originally told me that I would be in here for about ten days, but then yesterday they said not to be discouraged if I have to stay until the transplant in five more weeks. That would be a total of ten or eleven weeks in here. No bueno. But I've gotta look at the big picture. If I've got to be in here to stay healthy and make this worth it, I'll do it in a heartbeat!

Alrighty, well it's 4am, so I'm sure lots of this doesn't make sense and I probably skipped some details, but if I come up with anything too important I'll post again later.

Posted by Rachel at 3:25 AM

Thursday, September 23, 2010

Day 3 of my stay, or is it 4? No, no it's only Day 3...

So far, there's been no "real" news today. I had to get platelets, which isn't a big deal. I expected I would need them. I may need to get red blood tomorrow. I've been teetering around the "magic number" for a while.

The biggest issue we're dealing with is getting me on an IV feeding tube. I was on a 24-hour, nothing by mouth diet, and then a 24-hour liquid diet, and now I'm on a soft bland diet. I really can't eat anything without getting a stomachache. Any irritation or pressure I put on my bowels will worsen the infection and cause it to take longer to heal. I really don't need to deal with this any longer than I have to.

Normally they would have just put me on IV nutrition and there would be no problem, EXCEPT, for some other fun reason my bilirubin level is extremely high. (which is something in the liver, you'll have to look it up. It's important but I was paying more attention to my hunger pain) All I know is it's the same thing that makes newborn babies have jaundice, and it makes me have a yellow face and yellow eyes. (Yep, it's creepy). They say that with the level my bilirubin is at, if they start the IV nutrition it will become toxic. I also think it has to do with that fact that for some reason my liver is inflamed on top of all this, but I'm no doctor.

SO, moral of the story, I'm starving, but I can't eat and I'm already sick of this place. BAD sign! We were "kinda" hoping that being in the hospital would help me put ON weight, so far that's not looking' so good.

Posted by Rachel at 10:43 PM

Friday, September 24, 2010

Jealous

We're having another benefit at Dublin Square tonight. I really wish I was well enough to attend this, but since I can't, you guy's all go and have a good time. Also please tell the beautiful, curly haired princess that Mommy loves her. It sounds like a lot of fun and my mom has been talking about it non-stop for weeks. There's gonna' be raffles, live auction, a band, face painting, a coloring contest and jewelry making for the kids. Plus you get to eat at Dublin Square, which I hear has great food!

Hope everyone has a good weekend. I am about to get some stomach meds that will probably put me to sleep for a while.

Posted by Rachel at 2:23 PM

Saturday, September 25, 2010

Sick.

I am so sick of this place. I am sick of this bed. I am sick of this room. I am sick of the bathrooms with the tiny "hat" I have to pee in. I am sick of pulling around a pole everywhere I go. I am sick of not seeing my daughter. I am sick of being away from my dog. I am sick of not working. I am sick of not being at my house. I am sick of not being able to drive. I am sick of being weak. I am sick of symptoms. I am sick of no one being able to fix me. I am sick of getting medicine to fix what medicine did. I am sick of not being able to eat what I want, but simply what I "can handle." I am sick of needing "benefits" and "donations." I am sick of the word "eventually." I am SICK of being SICK!

UGH!!!!!!!

Posted by Rachel at 3:25 PM

Tuesday, September 28, 2010

Sorry I've been gone...

I've been slacking in the blog department the past few days and I apologize, but I have been a mess and it's been hard to focus enough to put together a post. After going a total of ten days without eating really anything other than 1-3 BITES of food a day and not being on IV nutrition during that time, I was very, very sick as you can imagine.

They finally were able to start my IV nutrition last night at a very low rate and I didn't really notice a huge difference, but my stomach isn't growling every ten minutes either. I'm a little better today though. They added some medicine for stomach pain relief and told me I can be a little more liberal with my pain medicine. It's good for me. Tonight they are going to up my IV nutrition so by tomorrow I should be doing good in that department. I have already been told by all of the nurses and doctors that have been in today that I am getting my color back, so it must be working some. Yesterday was my worst day in a while, so when they told me that night they would start the IV nutrition I was so happy. I was getting so weak from not eating that every time I stood up I was afraid that I would just collapse. Not to mention I was out of my mind, literally hallucinating. I told my husband about a conversation we had about our dog that never actually took place. That was kind of scary to know.

I did get a fever twice during the night last night, so we are worried I have some sort of stomach bug. Hopefully not since I haven't had a fever since noon, but overnight will be the real tell-all, I suppose. I have started throwing up the past few days, and my mom said a couple people at home are sick with a stomach thing too.
My doctor also said that my WBC looks like it is about to start rising. I guess there are some indicators they can see in the blood work before anything actually starts growing. It will be pretty slow over the next several days I'm sure, but once that starts to happen all of my little issues will one by one start to get better. Then we can go home. THANK GOODNESS.

Posted by Rachel at 6:10 PM

Friday, October 1, 2010

Hooray!

Well I had a sonogram of my...I don't know something this morning to make sure my infection and whatever else I had messed up was healing. Can you tell I pay the utmost attention when I don't feel well? Everything came back good, and my doctor said he felt comfortable taking me off all but one of my antibiotics. I was on five. He also said by the looks of my blood count today, he felt I was pretty well recovered from the chemo I got a few weeks ago. He took me off my IV feeding since I've been eating okay the past few days. I told him I would eat more if I were actually hungry, but IV nutrition kind of takes care of that. The only problems I still really have are some mouth sores that are trying to heal and some persistent leg and hip pain. Nothing major. He said as long as everything stays the same overnight and I feel up to it, he doesn't see any reason why I can't go home tomorrow. Woo Hoo! He is going to come by in the morning to check on me; if all is well we will get discharged! I am trying not to get too excited, just in case, but it's hard. I have never been in the hospital this long and I was most certainly NOT prepared for it. Twelve days is a REALLY long time.

My little princess came to see me today and I couldn't have been happier to see her. When she was home last night with Shawn, she ended up getting really upset and crying about how much she missed me, and our dog Corby. He is at my brother's while I am in here. She is very much a creature of habit and eventually when she can't be in her routine, it gets to her. Plus, she just plain misses her Mommy, dang-it! She just wants us all home as a family. You can imagine that broke my heart and made me miss her even more than I already did. When she got here today, I could feel how much we missed each other because pretty much the whole time she was here she was snuggled up in my bed with me; just like when she was a baby. It felt good to rub her head and feel her curly little locks between my fingers. Sometimes you forget just how truly amazing it is to be a parent. There is no love on earth like the love between a parent and their child. I just absolutely thank GOD for her each and every day. I am the luckiest Mommy ever.

When she is here I don't like her to get the impression that the hospital is this terrible place where Mommy is while she is sick. She never comes to see me when I'm in real bad shape, and when she is here I show her all the perks of being in the hospital. Like the cool bed that goes up and down and how if I want something all I have to do is push a button, ask for it, and like magic a nurse delivers it. I think she forced down two juice cups and an applesauce just so we could call and ask for more stuff. She was also pretty impressed by my snack collection from days of saving my cookies, or Jello, or whatever side I ordered from my lunch tray. I'm fairly certain her impression of the hospital right now has mostly to do with a GIANT playroom, all the snacks you can eat, and Mommy getting to sleep in a cool bed. The only bad things she sees is the giant pole I carry around and the fact that I pee in a little hat. I don't think that's too bad.

She got to go to Nana and Pappy's tonight (Shawn's parents), so hopefully she will have a great time and forget that she misses me so much. I am hoping by the time she comes back tomorrow, she can come home to me and it will be all better!

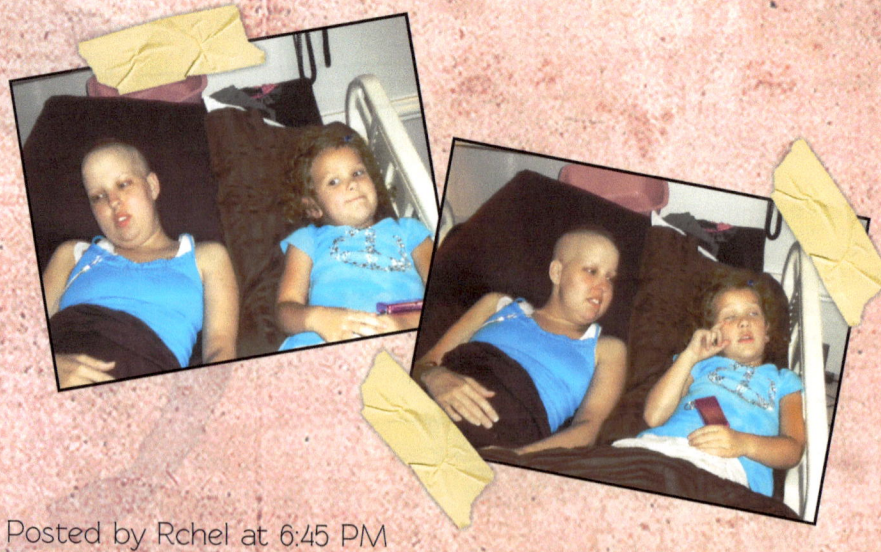

Posted by Rchel at 6:45 PM

Monday, October 4, 2010

Just Chillin'

So nothing exciting has been happening, which is a good thing. I got to come home Saturday morning and I have been pretty much at home relaxing and enjoying my family since then. Saturday night we went to watch Lexi cheer, but I'm not sure we have left the house other than that. My husband may have left to get food, but that's about it. Lexi is off of school today, so that is nice. I got an extra long weekend to spend with her after being gone from home for so long. I'm still really tired and sore, my stomach still isn't great, and my mouth has several mouth sores, but I'm happy to be home nonetheless. We are hoping I will be able to stay home and recover from now until the transplant. It will probably be 1-3 weeks until then. I am slightly nervous about the transplant just because I don't really know what to expect, and I know being gone from home that long is going to be very rough on everyone. Despite my little bit of apprehension, I am excited to get there. My theory is, the faster I start - the faster I'll be done.

I have a follow-up appointment with my doctor this Friday so I should have more of a timeline by then, at least I'm hoping so. From what I understand, as soon as they can get all of the pre-transplant testing set up and the donor to agree on a date to donate, we are ready.

Hopefully over the next few days my mouth and stomach will heal up, and the more time I spend away from the hospital bed, the less my body will ache. Shawn and I have been working on stretching and strengthening some of my muscles so I'm not a complete mess going into the transplant. He is like my own personal physical therapist!)

I will make sure to keep everyone updated as soon as I learn anything more about the transplant, as I know we are ALL anxious to find out when this is going to happen.

Here's to a boring week (for me at least)!

Posted by Rachel at 2:03 PM

Wednesday, October 6, 2010

We're getting closer.

It seems as though we're actually getting somewhere with the whole transplant thing now. (Not that we weren't getting anywhere before, it just seemed like it sometimes.) The transplant coordinator from the hospital called me yesterday to set up a meeting with one of the transplant doctors for this Friday morning. She said we will meet with her for about an hour and a half and go over all the details of the transplant; from pre-transplant treatment (chemo, radiation, etc) to all the after care, and everything in between. They also told me to make a list of questions because this would be the time to ask. After we meet with the doctor they will pick three dates they would like to do the transplant and send them to the donor. He will hopefully be able to donate on one of those days, and once he agrees to a date, we will be set and ready to go.

I'll have several days of testing done before we begin any more treatment to make sure all of my organs and such are in good enough shape to handle treatment, and also to make sure they give me the correct medicine to protect them.

I have more mixed feelings about all of this than I think I've ever had in my life. I am scared, but excited, but nervous, but anxious all at the same time. I am more nervous about being away from home, my daughter and being REALLY sick for a while than anything. The thought that this transplant won't work or something like that isn't even an afterthought of mine.

When I think about the transplant, I think about standing on the dock at my in-laws in the summer when I'm getting ready to jump into the lake and I know the water is going to be REALLY cold. You can't think about it, just close your eyes, jump in, and the hard part will be over before you know it.)

Posted by Rachel at 3:09 PM

Friday, October 8, 2010

Here goes...

I must say, after our meeting with the transplant doctor this morning, I had to come home and take a nap; it was information overload to say the least.

From what we learned today, we are expecting a very hectic next few weeks. The transplant team has sent my donor two dates to choose from that he can donate his marrow, and once he agrees to one of those dates we will then have our final transplant date. The earliest date they gave him was October 25th. Since it is possible he will choose that date and we will be in the transplant process in a little over two weeks, we are doing all of my pre-transplant testing starting on Monday. I have one or two appointments every day next week for tests, checking everything from my heart, to my liver, to my hearing, and everything in between.

It was obviously more than a little intimidating to sit and listen to a doctor tell me all of the things that could go wrong, not only during the transplant, but pretty much throughout the rest of my life from side effects; but even after all of that I still feel confident about transplant. It's gonna suck for awhile, but once it's all over I won't have to worry anymore.

Posted by Rachel at 6:55 PM

Wednesday, October 13, 2010

Moving right along

Things are really moving along quickly on the transplant front and I feel more and more confident about this each and every day.

Yesterday we met with the Radiation Oncologist, which actually made me feel more comfortable with the whole radiation thing then I ever thought I would. They went over the risks and everything, but she also explained to us that four days of radiation two times a day doesn't necessarily mean that I am being blasted with radiation. Yes, it is radiation so it still isn't fun, but it's not as intense of a dose as I was thinking. Since it is more of a reassure dose, rather than the first line of defense, they are able to give me less. We also heard back from the donor yesterday and he confirmed that he would be able to have his marrow harvested on November 3, which means my transplant day will be November 4. That is about a week later than we originally planned, but that means I get an extra week to recover and work on gaining some of the weight back I had lost.

This morning I had a follow-up biopsy of my bone marrow to confirm that I was actually still in remission. My doctor called a little while ago and said that my marrow was "clean as a whistle" and that my remission appeared to be holding well. There was talk about me possibly having to take a low dose of chemotherapy for a week since we added another week before transplant, but he said after today's test he is confident I will be okay without it. There was also some concern with my liver because during my last stay in the hospital, it was enlarged and they weren't quite sure why. I had a sonogram on Friday and some blood work to check the enzymes, and was told if it were still enlarged, I would have to do a liver biopsy to find out what was going on. (OUCH!) Looks like the sonogram and blood work both showed that my liver is back to normal. My doctor said he thinks it was just a lingering side effect from the steroid I had to take. (more reason to love the steroid).

and that it is not a long-term problem we need to worry about. THANK GOODNESS.

I have a few more tests this week and then we'll have our final pre-transplant meeting to go over all the results but so far so good!

Posted by Rachel at 4:03 PM

Monday, October 18, 2010

Great day, already!

It is still early and I have only been up for about an hour and a half, but today has already been one of the best days I've had in a long, long time.

I just got home from dropping Lexi off at school. I know that doesn't seem like anything exciting, but to me it was huge. Today was the first day since she started school that I have been able to get her there 100% by myself. I helped her get dressed, fixed her hair, made her breakfast, drove her to school and even walked her all the way to her classroom, alone. I have been too weak, sick, shaky, and so on to do any of that alone for the past three months. I am really excited about this coming week because I am feeling pretty good. I think the extra week I got by having the transplant pushed back is going to make a big difference in how healthy I am going into all of this. I have been able to eat pretty much like normal for the past few days, I've been getting a lot of rest, and most importantly I am gaining a significant amount of my strength back.

I also feel a lot better mentally. One of the hardest parts about all of this is being locked away from everyone. Well, yesterday my mom put together an early Thanksgiving lunch at her house and I got to see most of my family and close friends. Since I will be in the hospital on the real Thanksgiving and not able to eat most of the foods, I was so excited about this. It turned out great, tons of people I love came, and we had everything a regular Thanksgiving meal would have, including lots of leftover turkey!

I have about two, maybe three tests left to do this week, but other than that I think I have it easy for at least another seven days. I plan to enjoy my time and work on building my strength even more!

Posted by Rachel at 8:33 AM

150

Sunday, October 24, 2010

So close I can taste it.

I can't believe there are only three full days left until I go into the hospital. Thursday morning I'm having surgery to have my new central line placed and after that I will go to the transplant floor and stay there until I recover from transplant. Anywhere from 6-12 weeks! Next week is probably going to be spent doing laundry, packing and making sure all of my paperwork is in order. It's nerve racking to think that I am going to be out of pretty much everything for about a month. I just keep telling myself what my transplant coordinator told me "Short term discomfort for long term benefit."

Tomorrow afternoon is our final meeting with the transplant team before admission. Then I have an appointment to get the results of my neurophysiology test on Tuesday, and a fitting for my radiation lung blocks on Wednesday. None of those should take very long, but just enough to keep me busy I suppose.

I can't believe it's really right around the corner. I am just ready to get this going so we can get it behind us!

Get ready guys, 'cause it's just about show time! ;)

Posted by Rachel at 2:47 PM

Monday, October 25, 2010

Too ready?

Do you think it is possible I could be over prepared for the transplant? I didn't think so, but after today, I've gotta ask.

We had our second meeting with the transplant doctor today to discuss the results of all the tests they've been running on me lately, and also to have me sign that lovely seventeen page consent form. She ran through the whole form, which pretty much outlines anything that could possibly go wrong. Everything from the very likely to the rarest possible side effect. Sometimes those things are hard to hear, but I wasn't really phased by it. All of the results she had of my testing were good, I still feel great, and I know that almost anything could go wrong, but it's possible none of it will either. What am I going to worry about? Everything? That is almost impossible if you think about it. I would rather worry about nothing. I know that I'm about to walk into possibly the most difficult thing I have, or ever will experience in my life, and that is all I need to really know at this point. No matter how hard it is or how long it takes, it's all better than the thought of not being alive anymore because I am afraid to go through with it.

When we were getting ready to leave, the doctor said that she was a little worried about me because normally everyone breaks down during these meetings and I wasn't affected by it too much. I can't help it. I've done my research. I read the consent, and I decided to not be afraid of this. It feels right, and I feel like GOD is going to take care of me.

Also, just so everyone has an idea of what is going on, here is what my next week will look like.

Transplant day is considered Day 0, the preparative regimen is counted in "-", and every day after the transplant is counted as a " " day. My blogs from this point on will probably refer to days in this manner.

so you won't have to wonder what in the world I am talking about. Ex: Day 3 will be three days after transplant.

Thursday 10/28, Day -7: Surgery to have my central line placed, followed by admission to the transplant unit of the hospital.

Friday 10/29, Day -6: First dose of high dose chemotherapy (Cytoxan) and immune suppressant (ATG).

Saturday 10/30, Day -5: Second day of Cytoxan and ATG.

Sunday 10/31, Day -4: Rest day, third day of ATG.

Monday 11/1, Day -3: First dose of TBI (Total Body Irradiation) -given twice daily.

Tuesday 11/2, Day -2: Second dose of TBI.

Wednesday 11/3, Day -1: Third dose of TBI, harvest day for donor. (Marrow will be harvested from my donor in his home country and begin the trip to the US)

Thursday 11/4, Day 0: Fourth, and last dose of TBI, and TRANSPLANT DAY. The donor marrow will arrive to DFW sometime early in the day and will go straight to Carter Blood Center where they will begin to process it. Once it has been cleaned and the red blood cells removed, it will be couriered to the hospital where I will begin the infusion.

Posted by Rachel at 9:04 PM

Wednesday, October 27, 2010

So...

Tomorrow is the big day. Well, at least it's A big day. I go in to have my surgery and then be admitted to the transplant unit. It really hit me today and I have been packing and going through all of my things to prepare for my time away from home. I am ready for this (I think), but I am having a hard time knowing that I will be away from my daughter for so long. She started crying at the dinner table tonight when we were talking about it. She was really sad because I told her that I wouldn't be able to see my dog the whole time I'm gone. I think she felt bad for me, on top of the fact that she knows she will miss me.

My biggest decision right now is whether or not I should even consider trying to sleep tonight, because I can't imagine it will happen. I am too anxious/nervous, whatever you want to call it. I just need to get there so I can have a serious conversation with my doctor about exactly how much anxiety medication they can give. I'd be happy to go through the whole thing in a Xanax - induced stupor. ;)

Posted by Rachel at 9:25 PM

156

Thursday, October 28, 2010

So far, so good.

Well, I made it through my surgery. No big complications either. I guess they had some trouble getting the line where they wanted it and were concerned they punctured a vein, but once it was all said and done, a chest x-ray showed that everything was in the right spot with no internal bleeding or anything. I am obviously in some pain from the actual surgery itself, but it's not too bad. (Of course with the Morphin/Vicodin/Dilaudid combo they have me on, I would hope not!)

The line also isn't as bad as I was thinking. It's placed low enough that you can't see it when I wear a t-shirt, and the dressing that goes over it is much smaller than the dressing they usually have on me when my port is being used. The best part is I won't have a stupid needle stuck in my chest for 30 days, only plastic tubing.

I also have one of the nicest rooms on the floor, so I am happy about that. There are only two rooms up here that have large bathrooms, and one of them is mine. Most of the bathrooms in the hospital are so small I can hardly fit myself and my IV pole in there at the same time. I got the deluxe master bathroom here! Plus, there are only three rooms in the unit that have access to the visitor balcony, and my room is one of them. Which means, if anyone comes to visit me, I will be able to see them and talk to them through the window on the balcony. (Yes, kinda' like I'm in prison!) Most of the rooms don't have this so you have to go to a shared balcony sitting area to see visitors, which means I would have to be healthy enough to walk down there. Now I can just stay in my room!)

Posted by Rachel at 6:21 PM

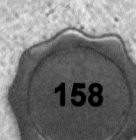

Friday, October 29, 2010

Day -6

Well, my first full day in the hospital seems to be iffy. I'm definitely going to have to adjust to all the rules they have for transplant patients. I feel like every time I turn around I realize that I have to throw my drink away because it has been sitting out for more than an hour, or I will think of something I want to eat and right before I ask my husband to run and get it, I realize I can't eat it!

When I woke up this morning I had a slight cough that hurt deep in my chest. They decided to do another chest x-ray to make sure there wasn't something going on with my lungs that was causing the pain in my chest. The x-ray showed that there is a small amount of air that leaked out of my lung into the cavity yesterday during surgery. The doctor said he thinks it was probably a tiny hole. Some air got out and then it was able to close itself back up. We are going to repeat the x-ray tomorrow just to make sure that it is either staying the same or getting better. Unfortunately, if it is getting worse they will have to go in and drain the air out with a chest tube. If there is one procedure that I would have to say hurts more than the rest, it would be that one. So let's hope not.

I also got my first dose of chemo earlier today and much to my surprise I did fine with it. I know it will kick my butt later once it starts killing all my cells, but hey, gives me one more decent day, right? Tomorrow is the second (and last) dose of chemo and then Sunday is my break day.

They had trick-or-treating in the lobby of the hospital today. I can't go down there, but I got a big bag full of stuff delivered to my door. Of course I gave it to Lexi and she was pretty excited about it! One of the perks of being at a kid's hospital I suppose. ;)

Posted by Rachel at 6:54 PM

Sunday, October 31, 2010

Next stop, radiation land

I had another pretty good day today. Got another chest x-ray done that looks like the air around my lung is decreasing. That is great news. The doctor told me this morning that if I wanted to put on the oxygen tube that may help it heal faster. So needless to say, I've been wearing it all day, why not try? Plus my nose is getting a steam bath. They hooked up a mini vaporizer thing to it so my nostrils don't get dry and bleed.

Lexi came to see me this afternoon in her Halloween costume. She was Super Girl. When they went trick-or-treating she brought her faithful side kick "Super Dog!" I am bummed that I wasn't able to be there, but I know she had a lot of fun. I'm not into all that walking anyway. I just want to dress her up and sit at the house passing out candy!

Tomorrow starts my four-day regimen of TBI (Total body Irradiation). I have to go twice a day, at 9am and 3pm. Not too sure what to think about it since I've never had it. Guess I'll find out when I get there. I do know that instead of a regular dressing over my central line, I have to wear some sort of gauze/ace bandage wrap/bra. I don't know.

As far as side effects go, I've been lucky. I have yet to throw-up. Most of the pain I am/was in, has been from the surgery and that's getting better. But leave it to me to get the fun, rare effects. The immunosuppressant I'm getting can cause hiccups, a very rare side effect. Well guess what, I had the hiccups for like four hours straight! Then of course there is my favorite, hallucinations. I have been dealing with terrible hallucinations the past few days. I just lay in bed looking into the bathroom, seeing it change into everything from a backyard, to a bedroom with sleeping babies, you name it. It's really weird, but it helps pass the time right? Haha.

Monday, November 1, 2010

Day -3

Just a quick update since I am tired and ready to go back to sleep. I had my first two rounds of TBI (Total Body Irradiation) today. It is a very weird process all together and I hope none of you have to do it. It doesn't hurt, you just lay still for about five minutes and listen to this giant machine make noise. Then, they turn you around and do it to the other side.

After my first round at nine this morning I didn't feel it too much. I was tired but that was more because I was up until 2am last night. There is a six-hour gap in between the doses of radiation they give you, so 3am was my next dose. I took a nap, woke up, and we were back at it again. Second round was a little faster because the machine was already set-up for me, which was good because I started to feel sick on the way over there. So, I hopped back up on the skinny little table and let the nurses push, pull and tug me into the exact position I need to be in. Then I just close my eyes and pretend it's not happening. It was harder this afternoon because I already felt sick and I know I have three more days of this. Shawn and I both broke down crying in the room, we then just sat there talking about how this will all be over soon enough.

I almost feel guilty myself, for my husband and my parents. I mean I know I'm the sick one here, but I don't have to stand by helplessly watching my daughter or husband suffer. I could not imagine that.

I feel like this transplant has been coming for ten years. I don't think I ever really believed that there was another way, but always hoped. The doctors knew best and they've got me into remission three times. Well, no more chances this time, we are gonna get this done with! I've got too much fight in me. I just have to crumble for a little while to remember that!

Wish me luck on TBI day 2!

(Okay, it was supposed to be a quick note!)

Posted by Rachel at 10:58 PM

Wednesday, November 10, 2010

Day +5, and I'm still alive!

Wow! I didn't intend to skip so much time in between posts.

Last week on Tuesday (11/3) in between doses of radiation, I stopped breathing and ended up being placed in ICU through Monday morning. Very Hollywood like with the "Code Blue" and everyone rushing in and getting a tube shoved down my throat. I had a lot of trouble while I was down there, but luckily for me I was on so much medication that I don't remember anything from those days. (So, if you want to know about my transplant, you'll have to ask someone who was conscious ;). It has been a struggle since I was sent back to my room here on the transplant floor. I definitely have a long road of recovery.

Posted by Rachel at 3:38 PM

Tuesday, November 16, 2010

Well I attempted to piece together an update from yesterday but apparently I fell asleep in the middle of typing it. So now you get a new one.

Day 10 (yesterday) is the day they finally start checking to see if you have any white cells in your blood. The doctor told me that typically you can start to see a white count at this time, but not to be worried if I didn't. A percentage of 0.01 or above was about average. My white count today was 1.3! She said that was an amazing white count for this early, and it shows that I got a good strong donor, and a good dose from him. They told me that in about another week I should have a white count high enough that I start feeling the effects of having a white count, as in I will start healing. My lungs will get better and a lot of the issues I'm having now should start to go away.

Now today (11), my white count has more than doubled in one day. It was 2.9 this morning. Yesterday was a miserable day for me, as I was achy, sleepy, and pretty much a mess. But making that many new white cells that fast would explain it. I actually slept the longest last night out of any night since I've been here. My mucus is loosening up ever so slightly which will set me on the path to recovery of my lungs, coughing and everything else. Hopefully everyday will be a little bit better any improvement is nice right now because I've just been kind of blah the past several days!

Posted by Rachel at 10:30 AM

Wednesday, November 17, 2010

Day +12

Well, I had a really tough evening last night as I have pretty much had a fever on and off since about five o'clock yesterday evening. They did some blood cultures to try and find out where it's from, and I am pretty certain it's an engraftment fever. I think this because it's not like a normal fever. I still get the "achy and I feel crappy" part of it, but not the "I'm freezing, but I'm actually burning up shiver." I've slept with a sheet and any contraption that could cool me off, including a cool pack. When I saw my WBC was at 5.7 today that confirmed it. My body is working hard and hopefully in the next few days I'll start feeling better.

Posted by Rachel at 11:06 AM

Saturday, November 27, 2010

Day +22

Hello everybody. This is Rachel's husband Shawn. I was hoping that I wouldn't ever need to post anything on here, but Rachel isn't doing too well and I figured I should let everyone know who is following her transplant through this blog. I won't be as entertaining as Rachel, but hopefully I make up with that with information.

A lot of things have happened in the past week that have led us up to right now and for the sake of time, I won't be able to cover every single detail. What I will do is cover the details starting from Thanksgiving. Rachel was admitted back to the ICU on Thanksgiving morning with difficulty breathing. The doctors were able to get her breathing under control very quickly, but decided to keep her in ICU for a few days of observation. At the time the doctors knew she had tested positive for a fungal infection (though they didn't know where); a virus called cytomegalovirus (CMV), and were suspicious she may have sinusoidal obstructive syndrome (SOS). On Thursday evening she began to have renal failure, so they put her on a machine called SCUF (slow continuous ultrafiltration), which is similar to kidney dialysis. Basically this machine is doing the job of her kidneys. On Friday morning, she began to have respiratory failure and the doctors had to intubate and put her on a ventilator. Right now she is not breathing on her own and is completely dependent on the ventilator. There was a little scare after the intubation when her blood pressure wasn't coming up, but they were finally able to stabilize that.

With all of the other problems she is having right now, they are not her biggest. I mentioned earlier the doctors were suspicious of SOS. Well they confirmed that yesterday. I'm going to put on my white jacket and try to explain what SOS is. There are a group of small capillaries that help her liver filter toxins from her bloodstream.

which of course is the main function of the liver. With all the chemotherapy she's had over the years, along with the recent radiation, those capillaries have been damaged and have become occluded causing a backflow of her blood away from the liver and back into her body. This has caused severe liver failure and has made Rachel "severely, critically ill" as the doctor said. In her condition, this is not reversible with the normal treatment for SOS, so they have sent out a request for an experimental drug called Defibrotide, which is still in clinical trials and not yet FDA approved. They expect to get this drug on Monday. There is still a low percentage of it working, but right now it is Rachel's only chance of survival.

It's looking pretty grim right now, but Rachel has always done well with her back against the wall. Obviously she has never faced anything close to the battle she has right now, but she's still hanging in there. I'm really scared, but I know my baby. Each time she's been low and seemingly hit a wall, she gets a little nudge from something: a medicine, fluids, etc. She'll take that little nudge and use it to keep fighting. I'm hopeful that this drug on Monday will be that nudge. Her wheels are spinning right now and I hope that Defibrotide will come around and give her a push.

Prayers are needed and appreciated right now. I know a good number of you reading this are in other countries and I can't imagine a better scenario than to have prayers flowing constantly to God from across the world. I know God is in the room. I can feel Him. Last night the person responsible for setting up Rachel and I, our friend Stacy, said a prayer asking God to "cuddle with Rachel as she lies in bed." I thought that was awesome and have no doubt that He is.

I will do my best to update everyone until Rachel can take the wheel again, which will hopefully be soon.
Sincerely,

Shawn Knight
Posted at 11:28 PM

Saturday, December 4, 2010

Day +29

Hey everyone, it's Shawn again. It's been a week since my last post and wanted everybody to know the latest update.

Today, a couple of hours ago, Rachel finally started the Defibrotide! It has taken so long because one of the criteria for receiving the drug was she could only be on one blood pressure medicine or "presser." Partly because the drug can lower your blood pressure, but mainly because she is receiving the drug as part of a "Phase 3" clinical trial and that was one of the requirements. The doctor found a "loophole" in the criteria that allowed Rachel to stay on two of the pressers because she just couldn't get completely down to one. The loophole was lowering the dose of one of the pressers to a level that could be considered a renal therapy drug and no longer a blood pressure drug. The oncologist who found the loophole said a couple of weeks ago that Rachel is "the toughest patient I've ever seen", and also that she "loves" Rachel. It's good to have the doctors on your side.

We were actually ready to give the Defibrotide yesterday morning, but her chest x-ray showed significant fluid buildup in her right lung and they started to get blood back from her breathing tube when they would suction out mucus. This made the doctors worry that she may have severe bleeding in her lung and therefore could not get the drug. In fact, the same oncologist almost started crying because she thought Rachel wasn't going to make it past the weekend. You don't usually want to see your doctor almost cry when talking about a prognosis, so I did worry a little, but still found myself comforting the doctor when she hugged me by reminding her that Rachel is still breathing. Of course, Rachel started getting better that afternoon and has steadily improved on everything but liver function, which is okay because the cavalry arrived two hours ago!

I do want everyone to understand that the Defibrotide could actually hasten her passing away. The drug can cause enough internal bleeding that it would be irreversible. There is about a 10-20% chance of this. Also, the drug may just simply not work. Other trial studies have shown an improvement on the percentage of turnarounds from SOS with this drug, but it was still at only 25%. However, having said that, the doctors and I agreed that she needs it because without it, she would run out of fight and wouldn't be able to reverse the SOS. I have a good feeling that even if it helps just a little, Rachel will do the rest. We should know in a few days if the drug is helping. I'll try and update Rachel's blog again then.

Keep praying and never underestimate my baby. She's one of a kind and a full recovery wouldn't really shock those who know her well. Thank you for the continued support.

Shawn

Posted at 11:54 AM

Tuesday, December 7, 2010

A Day That Will Live in Infamy

For those of you who have not heard, Rachel Susan Knight passed away today at 2:55 am in the ICU department at Cook Children's Hospital.

I've been reading all of the emails, text messages, and Facebook comments, and I've also been thinking about all the nurses and doctors who came by this morning to pay their respects to Rachel. I realized that Rachel has met the ultimate goal of life. If God had one goal that He would want each person to meet, it would be to leave the world a better place than before they entered it. Rachel always met her goals and this is her biggest accomplishment ever. No one who knew anything about my wife could argue that this world isn't better because of her.

She was always so humble and would get embarrassed whenever I bragged about her, but how could I not show off how wonderful my wife was? She was by far the better half in our relationship, although I did my best to keep up. Many people have told me how much our love has inspired them, and although I agree that our love was that of a fairy tale, it seemed so effortless and natural that I try to be humble when I hear this. Loving her was not this difficult challenge that I deserve praise. She made me stronger, happier, calmer, funnier, nicer, and just better than I ever would have been without her. She was my world, and I will try to go on and be as happy as I can for her although continuing through life without out my soul mate to lie down next to me every night will be my greatest task yet. I only have half of my heart now, and it is aching incredibly.

Thank you so much for everyone's continued support and encouragement. I can assure you that Rachel received much happiness from this blog. We loved looking at how many people from all over Texas, the US, and the world were reading her story. I hope you were inspired by her words, or at the very least amused by them. God bless all of you, and don't worry about Rachel, we all know she's in Heaven. Right before she passed away, I prayed to God that if there were any little Maltese puppies running around up there, that I would appreciate it if He gave one to Rachel because she missed her Corby for a long time. I also prayed that if there are any little girls up there who could use a good Mommy, Rachel is the best one I know and she would love to continue the job. I have no doubt that my prayers were answered and because of that, I know my sweet baby, my love, is in well...Heaven!

Shawn Knight

Posted at 8:34 PM

www.ingramcontent.com/pod-product-compliance
Lightning Source LLC
Chambersburg PA
CBHW042043290426
44109CB00001B/7